THE MOVIE OF THE WEEK

A M E R I C A N   C U L T U R E

Cutting across traditional boundaries between the human and social sciences, volumes in the American Culture series study the multiplicity of cultural practices from theoretical, historical, and ethnographic perspectives by examining culture's production, circulation, and consumption.

Edited by Stanley Aronowitz, Nancy Fraser, and George Lipsitz

THE MOVIE OF THE WEEK

PRIVATE STORIES
—
PUBLIC EVENTS

Elayne Rapping

American Culture, Volume 5

University of Minnesota Press
Minneapolis • London

Published by the University of Minnesota Press
2037 University Avenue Southeast, Minneapolis, MN 55414
Printed in the United States of America on acid-free paper

Library of Congress Cataloging-in-Publication Data

Rapping, Elayne, 1938–
   The movie of the week : private stories/public events / Elayne
Rapping.
      p.   cm. — (American culture ; v. 5)
   Includes bibliographical references and index.
   ISBN 0-8166-2017-2
   ISBN 0-8166-2018-0 (pbk.)
   1. Television broadcasting of films—United States.   2. Television
broadcasting—Social aspects—United States.   3. Television and
women—United States.   I. Title.   II. Series: American culture
(Minneapolis, Minn.) ; v. 5.
PN1992.8.F5R36   1992
302.23'45'0973—dc20   92-3187
                                                                CIP

Contents

For J.

Preface

When it comes to made-for-TV movies, people seem to fall into two distinct categories: those who love them and those who hate them. The latter category is far more vocal and therefore more visible. It is almost de rigueur for TV critics in daily newspapers to dismiss TV movies as trashy, sentimental, sensationalized tear-jerkers plagued with everything from wooden acting to poor production values. Those who disagree are seldom heard from, for obvious reasons. The verdict, in middle- and highbrow circles, has been so uniformly negative that it takes a certain amount of nerve to dispute it publicly.

What is more surprising than the public assent to the dismissal of telefeatures is the corresponding (tacit) judgment of media theorists who have in recent years done so much to rescue other forms of popular culture from the poor repute in which they have been held. Soap operas, both day and prime-time varieties, sitcoms, and talk shows all have received sophisticated, sympathetic critical attention, while TV movies—even when they are far more serious and intelligent—have received little.

This is very odd, it seems to me, because the TV movie, more often and more forcefully than any sitcom, for example, probes serious issues from a socially critical and informed perspective. Perhaps that is the problem. It is a form that is self-consciously serious in an age when irony and sarcasm are thought to be the appropriate attitudes toward political and social problems.

Self-consciously "arty" series like "thirtysomething" are embraced by those educated sophisticates at whom they are obviously aimed, those who share the distanced, ironic, self-reflexive stance of the characters and producers. On the other hand, those who have studied more naively artless forms like the sitcom and soap opera with so much sympathy and intelligence have had to take a different tack. Using sophisticated textual and ethnographic methodologies, scholars have discovered intricate subtextual elements in popular texts and equally sophisticated "against the grain" reading practices employed by fans that allow for readings and uses that are "oppositional" and potentially even liberatory. The theorists who develop such analyses position themselves at a distance from the viewers they study as well as from the texts themselves, in this case.

TV movies are not as easy to look at from either perspective. They are not self conscious enough to be considered deliberately hip, nor are they silly or implausible enough to be good objects of against the grain reading. They are old-fashioned stylistically and quite blatant in their moralistic, social messages. They use—and assume that their viewers buy into—the hokey realist conventions that have by now been thoroughly unmasked, deconstructed, and discredited by cultural theorists as bearers of falsely "naturalized," mythologized versions of social reality.

In deciding to write a book about TV movies, I had to choose a stance as an author as well as a theorist. The positions taken by most of the best television analysis today do not quite fit my purposes. For one thing, I consider myself part of the audience for whom TV movies matter. I consider them an important element in the broad public discourse about issues of public values and policies. By virtue of their emotional power, they are, I think, particularly significant elements in this discourse because they draw and move so many members of the viewing public—which, of course, is synonymous with the public itself in its general, political sense. In positioning myself as a conscious member of that broad public, I write from an authorial stance that is different from, or at least more complicated than, scholarly work that assumes a narrower, more professional context. This is unavoidable given my purposes.

I write about TV movies because I think they matter. They—along with any number of other, mostly print, media products—play a role in determining what and how we, as a nation, construct and conceptualize matters that affect us collectively. I watch them because of this and because they hold my interest more than most TV genres. (The two reasons obviously overlap.) I am not talking about all TV movies, to be sure. I'm not even talking about most TV movies. The movies I find significant, and the ones I have singled out to analyze, are actually a relatively small percentage of all telefeatures. Still, in relation to other genres, the percentage and sheer number of TV movies that resonate with personal and social meaning and warrant thought and debate are surprisingly large.

TV movies are unique in network television. For one thing, they are a television invention, not a leftover from radio. They were invented to fill a certain role and their success in filling that role has been greater than expected by the networks; therefore their role has grown as have their numbers. They were invented, specifically, at the time when television had ceased to be a novelty and the weekly schedule had become routine, to be special events that could be promoted heavily as out of the ordinary, "must-see" material.

When it turned out, as we shall see, that the most successful of the TV movies were those that tackled socially vexing, controversial subjects (*Brian's Song* was the first blockbuster), their importance to the networks grew. Now they could be used as cultural capital in television's battle for serious attention—thus their somber, pseudodocumentary tone and style (and their refusal, with obvious exceptions, to be ironic, cute, or intentionally silly).

From the early 1970s on, movies of the week became a TV staple, regularly scheduled "special events" touted as dramatically superior to series fare. Most importantly, they were presented as socially important documents, on the cutting edge of public debate and, in fact, a focal point for engaging us, as a nation, in debates in a much larger public sphere—in the real social world.

Subjects like slavery (*Roots*), domestic violence and incest (*The Burning Bed* and *Something about Amelia*), nuclear war (*The Day After*), AIDS (*An Early Frost*), corporate pollution (*Lois Gibbs and the Love Canal*), and many others all were given dramatic representation first on a TV movie. *An Early Frost*, in fact—and this is fairly common—is still probably the best and most serious treatment of AIDS in popular media. That these movies could be heavily promoted as major public events and then followed up with televised discussions among "experts," news reports, and information about how to learn more and get help made them more than mere entertainment devices. They crossed the line between fiction and fact, between drama and information and entered the realm of important social discourse not indirectly, through movie reviews, but quite directly through channels normally reserved for "real-life" events. But of course they are real-life events; they are public happenings around and through which major controversies are struggled over and negotiated. They participate in processes of social change, in a public sense, even as they affect us as viewers in our own understanding and attitude toward issues and in our discussions and actions in other parts of our lives.

In this book I am going to demonstrate their importance as well as their strengths and weakness, their power to facilitate change, and their tendencies—because they are part of an essentially stabilizing, conservative institution charged with keeping order and preserving the status quo—to restrict change. In other words, I am going to show how the institutional and historic factors that produced and shaped this form work, and then analyze the major forms of the genre in aesthetic terms and also in terms of the social implications of their economic and political contexts. The purpose of this book is to help viewers appreciate, from an informed and critical perspective, how TV movies work—for good and ill—and to see themselves as active viewers who, in watching a movie of the week, are participating in an important public event that calls upon them to make judgments and perhaps even, as a result of viewing, considering, and discussing, to act upon those judgments.

My audience, then, is the general television audience. That audience, however, is diverse, and it includes viewers with an endless variety of agendas. Not all viewers watch TV movies with the seriousness I describe. Most probably do not. But my intent is to be persuasive in changing less serious relationships to texts, to move readers to think differently about the movie of the week. I have chosen TV movies because, more than any other fictional form, they call upon us to think and act as citizens in a public social sphere. Moreover, they do this in a way that (for reasons we will discuss) links our personal domestic lives to our public ones. They represent a world in which father (actually it is usually mother) knows best about things that go beyond teaching children lessons of private morality. They show fathers and mothers tackling the large questions of their times and acting publicly, surprisingly often, as social agents.

In defining my projected audience I am including everyone who watches TV movies for whatever reason and in whatever critical frame of mind. There are infinite agendas with which we come to any particular TV program and infinite ways in which we might watch and receive them—sometimes more than one at a time. We may watch a single show with several different ways of thinking about what we see operating at once. We may watch it at two different times, in two different contexts, and have very different experiences. In my case, for example, I have been watching TV movies for quite a while as a fan, a college teacher, and a critical and scholarly writer.

Still, my primary stance in writing this is that of a public intellectual, a writer who wishes to engage a large public with a common stake in public life and in public media. And all who read this book, whatever their reasons, will be addressed as though they were part of that broad public because I believe that is the key position from which to consider television.

Since I am an academic and this book is published by a university press, it is obviously addressed to an academic audience and written in the context of current theoretical work on media texts. However, as I have said, that is not the only, or even the most important, contextual arena in which I position myself. In fact, it is part of the strategy of this book—the answer to my earlier question of what stance to take in writing it—to address my academic colleagues as members of the same larger public as the general audience because we do in fact inhabit that sphere and we have a responsibility to be aware of that fact when we write about things—like mass media—that have enormous social consequence.

Media studies is now a major academic field and it has, rightly, a lot of influence through its access to students and to certain segments of public discourse and publicity. There is no way that I could write about TV movies without addressing the monumental amount of often brilliant work that is now being done by scholars in teasing out the many ways in which TV texts "mean" and "signify," and in which viewers process them and make sense of them. Indeed, this book is indebted to so many scholars and theorists that I could not possibly name them all. I have incorporated a great amount of theoretical work into my thinking, although I have often found myself in disagreement with certain major tendencies and troubled by broader implications. Therefore, the thrust of this book is often at variance with the direction of other work on similar subjects. Most noticeably, I do not use the theoretical jargon common to academic writing on cultural matters even when it is implicit in the substance of my work because I find it often distracting to my purposes, and because it puts off those who are seriously, but not professionally, interested in television.

Because of the complex way in which I see this book existing in the realm of public discourses, I have written a special chapter, the introduction that follows, specifically to address theoretical and methodological matters, to place myself and the book in the current theoretical debates and endeavors to theorize media. It is primarily an attempt to speak to other scholars and explain what I am doing, what I am not doing, and why. It touches a variety of theoretical and methodological issues that will not necessarily be of interest to general readers for whom television matters because it is an important part of their everyday lives and because they like it and are interested in understanding it. The rest of the book deals with TV movies in a style that incorporates theoretical assumptions and methods, but uses a popular style and vocabulary to explain these things. Feel free to skip this introduction if you are not concerned with academic theory and research.

Chapter 1 describes the history of TV movies in the context of film history and of television as an industry. Chapter 2 presents the form as a genre with formulaic structural elements that serve certain aesthetic and social needs and analyzes several typical, not necessarily particularly interesting, examples. Chapters 3 and 4 deal with the most frequent, most significant kind of TV movie, the one that addresses women's issues from a decidedly female (if not feminist) stance and explains why women and feminism are particular concerns for the genre. Chapter 5 uses the same techniques to analyze the other important kinds of TV movies, those that represent events in history and those that address matters of race and class, another thing more common in TV movies than elsewhere on television. Finally, there is a brief afterword in which I speculate on the future of the form.

Introduction

Contextualizing Cultural Studies

This is a book about an important public sphere within which social meanings and myths are constructed and circulated: television. It interrogates the role and workings of one particular fictional genre, the made-for-TV movie, within the context of that public sphere. It assumes that commercial television, in its modes of production and of consumption, matter very much in our common political life. It assumes that TV movies, in particular, matter because they operate in a unique way as discursive sites upon which representations and ideologies of "the family" are struggled over first in the text itself and then in the larger public sphere of social and political relations, by virtue of the form's special position among popular narrative texts and its intertextual relations to other discursive structures—news broadcasts, media critique and debate, formal and informal gatherings in which the movies and their topics are discussed. Most importantly, perhaps, it assumes that an understanding of the textual practices of one form of television narrative, within the public sphere of the medium as a whole, may lead a bit closer to a model of how the media intervene among actual social conditions and power relationships. It is an attempt to map out the contextual arena within which television exists and to explore the interconnections among texts, productive institutions, and audiences (understood in a particular way) as one very small part of a larger, much-needed investigation of how change might come about in a postmodern world in which electronic representation has unprecedented authority.

The roots of this book go back some twenty years. Traversing those years, in retrospect, appears to have been a journey to another universe entirely, one in which assumptions about cultural critique, social and political experience, and the relations between them have been transformed. In the late sixties, when I began writing about television, there were no academic departments, disciplines, or journals addressing media and popular culture as objects of interrogation or theory. The impetus for taking popular culture seriously as an object of study was political and practical. It grew out of the ideas and strategic goals of the New Left.

In this it was not different from, although it was far less developed than, the work of the founders of the Birmingham School of Cultural Studies in Britain at about the same time. In fact, these activist/scholars—especially Stuart Hall and Raymond Williams —became, along with Antonio Gramsci and the Frankfurt School theorists, our primary influences. While they were working within a university structure, they were very much an oppositional force within academia, as Stuart Hall has recently reminded us (1990). Hall and his colleagues, like my own friends in the far less sophisticated American New Left, had a political agenda, which was to contest existing power relations. Hall describes this agenda as "a Gramscian project" motivated by the ideas that "we were a tiny part of a hegemonic struggle" and "that the questions we were asking were of central relevance to the questions through which hegemony is either established or contested" (Hall 1990, 17–18). The interest in popular culture, for them and for us, was motivated by a realization that this culture—broadly understood to include the popular arts as well as "lifestyle" practices—was the site of ideological struggle and that such struggle had actual consequences. "It was not possible to present the work of cultural studies as if it had no political consequences and no form of political engagement," Hall says of those times, "because what we were inviting students to do was what we ourselves had done: to engage with some real problem out there in the dirty world . . . to try to understand how the world worked" (17).

This early work remains seminal to the now established academic field of American cultural studies. But for many reasons connected with historic, political, and social changes in this country, its link to the kind of political engagement Hall describes is less clear.

For one thing, we in this country have never had the kind of political environment, informed by a tradition of class struggle, that informed the British New Left. We in the American New Left were young and largely from a middle-class background. We inhabited a naively utopian subculture that at the time seemed far more "revolutionary," more capable of sustaining itself and engendering change, than it turned out to be. Our ideas about the links between theory and practice were romantic, and they were influenced by the remarkable experiences of an unusual generation at an unusual time.

Those were pastel-tinted, soft-focus days when no one had yet teased out the many strands of confusion and complication inherent in our ideas about cultural politics. Issues of difference had not been raised. Most of us innocently spoke in totalizing generalizations about Women, People, the Working Class. Subjectivity and identity were similarly not issues we thought about, much less worried over. We had not yet heard the poststructuralist/postmodernist news about the death of the bourgeois self and its master narratives and the corresponding decentering and fragmentation of publics and audiences. We had no idea, in 1968, that that very year would soon be the tag for something far more incandescent in significance than the Democratic convention in Chicago; that it would mark, for many influential people, the start of the postmodern era.

But almost immediately all of these turns were upon us. The implications of our own rudimentary cultural theory, aided by the coming of so much European theory to our shores, suddenly emerged as awesome and politically intimidating. There were a million new questions and problems to consider before we could assert much at all about texts, audiences, and—most certainly—political action. By the time we absorbed all of this, the world had changed. We entered a time of political conservatism in which the utopian dreams of the sixties were first eclipsed and then nostalgically historicized by a generation too young to remember them. During this period, the seventies and eighties, as Douglas Kellner notes, "many former 1960s radicals turned . . . to theoretical work, directing their political energies toward new work in theory. . . . For many this involved abandonment of the radical perspectives of the sixties" (Kellner 1989, 23). They also got older and entered the professional work force, mostly—those who took this theoretical turn—as academics, of course.

The importance of this material social development is most apparent in the recent media and right-wing hysteria over "political correctness" and "multiculturalism." The insertion of postmodern theories and discourses into the curriculum and their attendant effects upon accepted beliefs about what constitutes knowledge and culture have had an obvious impact on the university as workplace, if nothing else. But in the process the focus of radical activity has shifted, to a great extent, from practice to theory, from the public realm to the more narrowly textual.

And so, I think, we find ourselves in a strange, contradictory moment. Cultural theory has never been more sophisticated, more elegant, more ambitious in scope. The understanding of artistic and cultural production and consumption is theoretically vast, impossible to avoid or dismiss. It is no longer possible to talk about texts or audiences in the naive, totalizing, naturalized ways in which we once did. The old assumptions have been permanently unmasked—to the greater good of all—and we who write about media must do so, implicitly or explicitly, in the context of the new theory. Texts, interpretive, social, and cultural practices, historic events, and subject identities and positions all appear in new nakedness as constructs in the service of local interests.

The problems inherent in this rather lopsided relationship between theory and practice are very much in the air these days. More and more scholars are raising questions about the implications of some of the most dominant theoretical practices. To take just one example, as I write this introduction I am impressed by the fact that the current issues of two feminist journals to which I subscribe, *differences* and *Genders*, include articles that discuss this problem. The concern with difference, with the deconstruction of totalizing narratives and the recognition of plurality, which at one historic moment served progressive ends, may in some practices today represent, in Linda Gordon's words, "a depoliticizing, even a conservatizing of our work" (1991, 92). Similarly, Kathleen Jones asks, "If we displace sovereignty—the desire to control difference by representing it as unity—what happens to the coherence of the feminist project?" She is speaking about the political project of feminism, the belief in the relation between theory and practice, between material social conditions and theories about their representations. "If 'woman' is merely a myth that deconstructs itself into the plurality 'women,' then there is no longer any sense to be made of the statement 'exploitation of women' " (1991, 120–22).

These questions are real and important. Both Gordon and Jones are concerned about reestablishing a concrete connection between our interpretive practices as critics and scholars and the liberatory project that first moved us to develop them.

They, along with many other scholars, among them media theorists, believe there is a need to find "a basis to refound our social relationships" (Jones 1991, 123) and collective political identities. In other words, we need to reincorporate the original political agenda of women's (and, I would add, cultural) studies into our theoretical models and see what happens. Of course we cannot ignore all that has been learned. On the contrary, we need to use these powerful tools to correct the naive, superficial thinking of the sixties. As Jones says, "this does not mean that gender, class, race, and sexuality . . . dissolve into endlessly mobile, hence non-existent chimeras." It means that "we maintain analytic distance between them, as heuristic devices, and the lived, material reality through which they echo and are refracted" (Jones 1991, 123), a reality that demands that we find ways to generalize, to posit a common sense of political identity that unites, even as we keep in our mind our differences not only of race, class, and so on, but also of daily life and cultural practices and tastes. As Gayatri Spivak has argued, it is often necessary, for reasons of political strategy, to speak of "women" as though we believed in essentialist notions of gender and identity—all the while remembering that this is simply a political expedient—since this is the only way to fight sexism in the real world (Spivak 1990).

Introduction

"Audiences" and "Publics"

I raise this issue—discussed often in feminist circles in which the practical political project that informed the development of women's studies is still often discussed—because I think it applies to cultural studies as well and should be similarly discussed by cultural theorists more than it is. Certain tendencies in current media theory may be seen as similarly "conservatizing," in the sense that they no longer ask or answer questions about how actual oppositional forces and practices may develop in ways that are collective and therefore capable of challenging existing power differentials and relationships. In particular, much of the work being done by those who study "audiences" and interrogate the uses and gratifications of the various social practices of daily life seems, while fascinating and important for what it teaches us, to veer a bit far afield of the original political mission of cultural studies.

David Sholle, in a critique of the notion of "resistance" in audience reception theory, pinpoints the ways in which this work puts cultural studies at risk of "losing sight of its past." That past, he reminds us, "as conceived by Raymond Williams and the followers of the Birmingham School has always defined itself . . . against the deterministic strain in critical approaches" that posit "the overwhelming power of the media to determine social and cultural practices" (Sholle 1990, 88–89). While he sees that the "recent turn" toward the study of audience activity is very much in line with this rejection of deterministic theories, he rightly notes the danger in celebrating any and all kinds of "resistance" and "making do" on the part of audiences because it forgets to ask the crucial question: to what political end? "If the activity of audiences is simply a matter of 'making do' then why look at these activities as having any importance at all?" he asks (102). A similar question arises about the much-heralded liberatory potential of "pleasure" in the consumption of texts (Ang 1985, Fiske 1987).

When this kind of work on cognitive practices endeavors to answer the question of political consequences, very often a notion of some kind of temporary or momentary resistance is put forth as politically meaningful. Thus Janice Radway states that "romance reading temporarily transforms patriarchal relations"

(Radway 1984, 133). But what is the *ultimate* consequence of such "temporary" transformations (if indeed a transformation can be thought of as temporary at all)?

It is true of course that such momentary experiences or feelings may lead to actions that are in fact materially transformative. But which feelings, in which contexts? And which actions, in which very complex sets of contextual forces of other kinds? Aren't these the questions we need to be asking? For if we slide over them, we have said very little of consequence. In fact, as Sholle points out, one actual consequence of Radway's "temporary transformations" may well be to lead to more and more romance reading, as a psychological form of relief from actual material conditions.

It is this kind of discussion that reception theorists, focusing on differences among viewing practices, do not allow. The most sophisticated examples, in fact, refuse to confront content issues as ideology or make political or aesthetic judgments. Lawrence Grossberg, in his extensive and clarifying work on rock music and its fans, goes furthest toward articulating these matters. His work is important because it moves us to the very edge of making political statements, to the very moment when the mediation between fan and text may, potentially, lead to some explicitly political action. He cannot go past that moment of potential action, of political choice and judgment, because he does not deal with the text itself. In fact, his treatment of this subject, based on postmodern theory, makes the issue largely irrelevant since matters of taste and style among rock fans are presented as infinitely varied and relative. "Different fans are likely to disagree over where the line is to be drawn [between what they do and do not consider 'real' or 'good' rock and roll] and it is rarely an issue entirely defined by musical or economical criteria . . . [it] is a matter of its affective power," he says, "of whether it is locatable within the affective economy of *the fan's* apparatus" (Grossberg 1984, 103, italics added). In other words, we cannot determine individual responses in terms of ideology nor can we assume any two fans will respond similarly even to explicitly ideological lyrics.

Grossberg is aware of this issue and confronts it directly, making sure to make no political claims for particular text/fan interactions. He carefully distinguishes between "affective empowerment," which the music may in certain instances produce, and actual political resistance. "It is the affective position of the fan that the apparatus empowers," he says, providing the possibility of power, but only the possibility. At this point, he goes on, "culture offers the resources which may or may not be mobilized into forms of hegemonic or oppositional popular movements" (103). But since each "fan" experiences her own kind of pleasure and empowerment, is "interpellated into the rock and roll apparatus" (103) at his own chosen site of demarcation of what constitutes "good" and "bad" rock and roll, or even rock and roll at all (as distinguished from mere pop), the argument ends here. We cannot say anything more about the conditions under which "oppositional movements" may form, about what kinds of experiences, what forms of "pleasure," at what particular historical sites of economic, cultural, and political intersections collective transformation may actually happen.

The problem here is not that we cannot answer these ultimate questions under any circumstances whatever, that they are simply unanswerable (although they may be, I suppose). It is that this kind of analysis leads farther and farther away from even asking such questions. It becomes so bogged down in private cognitive practices, styles, and tastes, so stuck in moments of affective empowerment or temporary transformations, that it becomes a kind of apology for not expecting anything more of us as political beings, for celebrating private pleasures based on infinities of difference for their own sake and, ultimately, redefining the word *political* to fit these inherently noninstrumental views of cultural use.

To return to the Radway example of romance reading, one possible political result of feeling liberated from an oppressive patriarchal marriage, even momentarily, might be—and this is itself a fairly trivial example except in the very personal terms of the reader's private life—that a woman decides to leave her husband and go to a women's shelter. It is more than a moment of cognitive recognition of her own situation and injustice that will lead to this, however. She will need, further, to be made aware of the existence of such a place within traveling distance from her home and, perhaps more importantly, to learn and believe that other women, as seemingly powerless as she feels, have made that move.

Having accomplished this much, we are still very far from structural changes that are collective, permanent, and institutional. We have not explained how the reader might gain a sense of political identity based on gender or, finally, how she might be brought into collective, organized, political movement. And yet, extreme as these suggested political goals may seem in this time of reaction, pessimism, and lack of organized political resistance of almost any kind, they are the only meaningful kinds of goals that can really be considered politically transformative. There is no way a theory of readership based on difference and private practice can do this. What is needed is a way to see popular texts and practices as single aspects of a holistic public sphere of discourse and action and readers as part of the publics that participate in such spheres in a variety of ways.

That so few theorists are asking these questions is a serious problem. It leads inevitably away from the original "Gramscian project" with which cultural studies starts. To be sure, the reasons for this subtle depoliticizing turn can be traced, legitimately, to the important insights upon which cultural studies was founded. Cultural studies tradition does indeed locate the site of political struggle within the text, and within the relation of audience to text in the private activity of constructing meaning. It also takes from Walter Benjamin the idea that the mechanical reproduction of artworks opens up democratizing space in the cultural sphere for the masses to engage in such struggles over meaning.

On the one hand, this means that textual producers encode dominant, hegemonic meanings into texts in order to gain this consent. On the other hand, of course, audiences have the power to resist these meanings in certain situations since they are always encoded in contradictory ways to ensure that consent may be achieved across a broad collective audience divided by many kinds of difference. But in using this model—and it is the model I am using in this book—it is necessary to remember the differential power relations between producers and audiences, especially if one is using a model of audiences in which difference and the privatized nature of reception are assumed. Any adequate theory of "resistance," then, must take into account the workings of the media industry itself, in encoding dominant readings, and must find some way to get beyond the atomized models of reception that now dominate.

The problem here is again very much the same as the one posed by feminists. How do we politicize our theories of audience behavior and interpretive practices? How do we adequately theorize audience relations to social and political institutions in ways that suggest activities that promote change? It seems to me the answer does not lie in the kinds of audience work now being done. We have accumulated an emormous amount of ethnographic material about viewer behavior and the minutia of everyday life practices. We have determined, through the work of scholars such as Ann Gray (1989), Dorothy Hobson (1981, 1982), David Morley (1987), Ien Ang (1985, 1991), Liebes and Katz (1986), and Andrea Preiss (1991) that, as Charlotte Brunsdon put it, "people watch television in heterogeneous ways" (1990, 65). But we have not been asking how they watch it in similar ways or, more to the point, how they receive and use it in ways similar enough to lead to potential changes in power relations.

Thomas Streeter rightly says, "The most salient form of resistance involves politicizing [differences], insisting that cultural differences such as language and tradition have more than personal private implications, that they call for major political and social change." In other words, we must think about resistance in a more public, politicized way. We must analyze texts in terms of their ability to "find common openings . . . and open up dialogue between different sub-altern groups aimed at altering power relations" (Streeter 1989, 29, quoted in Sholle 1990, 103).

In order to move in the direction Streeter suggests, it is necessary to speak as though certain things that are now theoretically obvious do not need to be repeated again. We assume here that just as the concept "woman" must be used in spite of its totalizing, essentialist meaning to make meaningful political statements, so must we use the concept of "audience" as undifferentiated mass. It is well known (Ang 1991) that the Nielsen ratings are a fiction, that the mass audiences they measure are constructs, and, moreover, that they are defined in ways that serve the needs of sponsors and networks, not viewers. Still, they do give us the only figures we have as empirical evidence that a "mass" of American citizens is participating in a common discursive and interpretive practice, in some meaningful sense, at one and the same time.

Indeed, in spite of all we know about the differences in the ways individual viewers receive and interpret texts, there is something commonsensical about acknowledging that there is still a dominant text we all recognize as the thing we have experienced. We may watch alone or in groups, we may tape a program and watch it in segments. We may rent a TV movie and watch it as a closed narrative, free of the "flow" effects of commercial and other textual interruptions. And yet, there is an idea of an entity called *The Burning Bed* that we can talk about in common because we have in our minds a sense of how it is in fact a recognizable, discursively describable entity (Brunsdon 1990).

Moreover, as Ella Taylor points out, the issue of audience differentiation, theorized by the networks as demographics, is understood to be important for economic reasons. Therefore, if you know, for example, that large numbers of "women" watch TV movies (and they do, relative to other segments of the public) you can be sure that, for commercial reasons, the networks and sponsors will be more concerned about including, as part of the ideologically contradictory and tension-filled narrative text, elements taken from feminist discourse (and, as we shall see, they do). On the other hand, since any network program aims to attract the largest number of viewers possible, the "heterogeneity of viewers must be simultaneously catered to with pluralistic images and glossed over with a more universal language" (Taylor 1989, 166).

Thus, the "dominant text" produced by the network exists as a unifying construct that, by virtue of the commercial demands of the industry, also exists as a heterogeneous, internally contradictory and polysemous one as well. We can then easily address the hegemonic workings of such texts in terms of the contradictory nature of the encoding process itself. Such a framework allows us to discuss the textual practices of television in terms of a verifiable mass public that is also, in politically significant numbers, partly understood in terms of difference.

In discussing Radway's comment on romance readers, I said that we had no way to know what, if anything, about their reading practices might lead them to engage in personal, much less political, struggle for change. I used as an example of such action a woman reader being moved to leave an abusive situation and go to a shelter. The TV movie *The Burning Bed*—a narrative in which one such woman, lacking access to a shelter, killed her husband and was acquitted—was watched by 75 million viewers the first night it was aired. It was then discussed and commented upon in news follow-ups that provided viewer information on institutions including shelters that help battered women. The case upon which the movie was based was that of Francine Hughes, and the legal defense used successfully in a domestic violence case for the first time—temporary insanity—was developed with the help of a defense committee formed and made up largely of socialist-feminists in the late seventies. This movie became a media event and also entered the public sphere of significant ideological discourse in ways that other cultural artifacts consumed in other, less public, contexts would not. In terms of immediate response, we know only what the popular press reported, and this information is surely personal and incomplete: the next day, at least four women killed their husbands and one man set his wife on fire. Using a different model, there is little one can make of these actions except that these individuals were "affectively empowered" through the viewing of this movie at a moment in which a variety of other forces intersected in their lives. What they did seems to have been related directly to the text of the movie. Were these "political" actions? One would have to say so. Were they "progressive"? The question is obviously absurd. Moreover, it is grist for the mills of the "effects theory" people with their openly conservative agenda to promote censorship.

In terms of affective empowerment, the movie had contradictory effects on only a handful of viewers. In terms of political significance, however, it is impossible to deny that this drama worked its way into a public consciousness in ways that—combined with any number of other textual and social interventions in the public sphere—have led to actual structural changes in the way domestic violence is handled. The governor of Ohio recently pardoned some 90 women who had been incarcerated for killing their husbands. The existence of shelters became public knowledge. The sexist treatment, by the police and courts, of domestic "squabbles" was put under public scrutiny and largely altered, at least in policy. And surely, over time, many women have been affected by the mediation of this movie into social and political realms. This is not to give this single movie more power than it can be known to have or, indeed, can possibly have had on its own. It is only as a single part of a collection of events, working across diachronic and synchronic lines in the realm of social reality, "causing" some things, reacting to others, that the movie can be credited with participating in a structure of causes affecting change.

In this example of how a TV movie may work as social intervention, I have focused on the texts—as opposed to audiences—as the central issue. This is because I believe that, as this example shows, the encoding process itself is more interesting and contradictory than is often assumed, and, more to the point, it is easier to evaluate politically. The focus on private reception has become lopsided in its tendency to ignore production. When production is put in a more prominent place in the equation, the nature of reception, and its social ramifications, appears in a broader, more easily politicized light. Moreover, we can say quite a lot about how TV texts are produced and how they arrive at their final textual construction, and what we can say is often easier to draw political conclusions from than private reception practices are. Indeed, *The Burning Bed* is a good example of a media event in the encoding of which the feminist movement, in its most politicized and organized form, was undeniably a participant. What happens after the encoding (the contradictions and tensions of which will be analyzed) and airing of the text is less clear. But, because we do have empirical information about production, I think it is particularly useful to construct a model of television as public sphere and audiences as publics involved in this public sphere not only as decoders of texts, but also as politically identifiable subaltern communities who have—symbolically and indirectly—participated in the production of texts in their roles as consumers and, in some cases, as actual oppositional political groupings.

Thus, the concept of oppositional readings—while obviously central to a view of the relationship between media and social change—is not sufficient to describe how popular texts may become sites of ideological struggle over meaning. Production is a slippery site fraught with contradiction and ideological struggle.

In failing to interrogate the workings of the networks and studios themselves, in falling into vague theories such as "the-author-in-the-text" (Fiske 1986), we fail to take this into account sufficiently. There are in fact writers, producers, directors, and performers who have their own agendas and varying levels of power to enforce them. What Lisa Lewis (1990) and Susan McClary (1990) demonstrate about the "intentions" and power to produce texts of performers like Madonna also holds true for certain producers of television narratives.

In fact, this is most particularly true of producers of TV movies because, as I will elaborate in the body of the book, TV movies offer opportunities for a kind of work not easily done elsewhere in television or film and therefore tend to attract from the start producers, actors, and writers with more politicized agendas.

But then, the Gramscian view of hegemony assumes as much. Indeed, even the much-maligned Frankfurt School theorists were far more sophisticated about this matter than they are now credited with being. It is common among poststructuralist and postmodernist theorists simply to dismiss these earlier theorists as "old-fashioned lefties" with simple-minded views about "manipulation" and "hypodermic theories of reception." But in fact, as Thomas Streeter points out, "Horkheimer and Adorno did not arrive at their pessimistic views because they failed to take into account social difference, plurality and resistance. Their despair should not be taken for an orthodox, mechanistic understanding of social domination. On the contrary, their fear was that plurality and difference has been thoroughly accommodated to the modern order" (1989, 16). From that perspective, individualized reading strategies, in and of themselves, are of little social consequence.

In our respect for difference, then, we must not lose sight of what still, for political purposes, must be spoken of as a dominant culture and a dominant, if contradictory and polysemous, text. The idea of public spheres, of which television is among the most important examples, is therefore heuristically useful. It allows us to posit a set of representations and textual practices existing in a common site within which a complex, shifting set of dominant and subaltern meanings are struggled over by an entire community with a broadly shared set of social terms and values understood to be at stake in the process of these negotiations. The term *public* is for my purposes more useful, then, than *audience.*

The public sphere construct also allows me to focus upon texts and their content, their actual relationship to a lived reality. I have chosen to focus on texts and meanings and, to a lesser extent, on the modes of texual production, of encoding—as separate from decoding—because it allows me to keep a focus on what about television is actually public and shared, at the point before issues of difference and reception take hold. It puts ideology, unashamedly, back into the center of the equation and assumes a direct relation between what is viewed and some at least partly corresponding version of "reality." It allows me to talk unselfconsciously about the truths, the values, the rights and wrongs of particular texts, to make aesthetic and political judgments (Brunsdon 1990) on the basis of this assumed (in some ways obviously naive) correspondence.

Such a concept of television as a public sphere, as "the structured setting where cultural and ideological contest or negotiations among a variety of publics takes place" (Eley 1991, 143) and whose "members understand themselves as part of a potentially wider public . . . 'the public-at-large' " (ibid.) is useful. In spite of its limits, its tendency to "fluctuate between being a facade of legitimation capable of being deployed in diverse ways and being a mechanism for controlling the perception of what is relevant for society" (Eley 1991, 67) it remains, as Alexander Kluge says, "the only form of expression that links the members of society who are merely 'privately' aggregated . . . by combining their unfolded social characteristics with one another" (Kluge 1988, 66).

Television is hardly a perfect model of democratic representation. Its separation from state and economic interference is attenuated, to say the least. Its willingness to include oppositional, subaltern voices is marginal. But it is not a monolithic totality. It succeeds more than other forums in hailing us as citizens with interests in common and in embodying a version of public debate on matters of common concern that has credibility and authority—in spite of questions about the quality of its mediation or its actual effects in terms of viewer behavior in the political as opposed to private arena.

Indeed, the only way to use the immense knowledge and theory we now have concerning interpretive and use practices in political ways is to begin asking how, or if, these practices fit into some such model. John Fiske says, at the end of a study of the ways in which television texts are in fact used in the course of a viewer's daily life in ways that are potentially "liberatory," that "if the popular did not connect—however indirectly—with the lives of those who are categorically subordinated in our society, there would be little point in studying it. Equally," he goes on, "if its emancipatory potential was never used to ease the material conditions of subordination, there would be little point in attempting to understand it" (Fiske 1990, 146). Just so. The concrete example he offers of how this works is that of a schoolgirl who says of "Cagney and Lacey," it "gives me the confidence in myself to know that I can do just as well as boys in sports" (141). This is important. But to go from playing softball to making larger changes in women's material and political conditions is a jump— one that requires a mapping out of a public sphere in which the articulation of a potential ability to participate in sports appears in conjunction with the other matrices of the girl's life and links them to that of all other girls sharing her subaltern position as part of a group experience of inequality that is understood in terms of gender identity politics.

Realism: The Revenge of the Depth Model

We live in a world in which "our experience is no longer whole: we are no longer able to make any felt connection between the concerns of private life . . . and the structural projections of the system in the outside world," says Fredric Jameson. And so, the role of media, of the "dream world of artificial stimuli and televised experience" (Jameson 1971, xvii), is all we have to talk about as common ground. This imperfect dream world is important because it "plays a large role in bridging or mediating the gap between our unrealized political ideals and our lived social relationships" (Mann 1990, 87).

TV movies are an important part of the televised dream world because they, more than other genres, construct dramas within which our "unrealized political ideals" are most explicitly represented and negotiated. Because these representations are constructed out of the conventions of naive bourgeois realism, one must be careful when speaking about their content, their social and political subject matter. Unless one is specifically deconstructing texts for the purpose of exposing the falseness of such realist representation, it is hard to discuss them without—to some extent—falling into the transparency fallacy, falling into language that can be understood as accepting at face value the naive reflection theory of representation, a danger that is as hard to avoid as it is theoretically discredited.

Since the 1950s, largely because of the work of Roland Barthes, it has been a truism that all texts are constructions, representations; that bourgeois narratives serve to naturalize history. Removing what is contingent and historical from representations "purifies them, it makes them innocent, it gives them a natural and eternal justification" (Barthes 1975, 143).

Television is particularly guilty of this sham because its narratives are constructed with the most naive and obvious realist practices. It "abolishes the complexity of human acts . . . [it] gives them the simplicity of essences, . . . does away with all dialectics, with going back beyond what is immediately visible . . . [and] organizes a world which is without contradiction because it is without depth" (Barthes 1990, 143). Since it is the dominant representational and discursive public sphere, it could not be otherwise. Realism is still the official cultural practice of all our institutions. It is the only commonly understood discursive and representational system.

As members of a common world, we need these common narratives and textual practices that try to explain our condition to us, no matter how inadequate they may be. They allow us to construct what Jameson calls "cognitive mappings" to approximate the world in which we must move and act. And these mappings, to the extent that they are comprehensve and socially useful, must be totalizing. To the extent that we share a world, we tend to share, also, a common cognitive map of that world. If television works as a public sphere better than other, more avant-garde cultural forms, it is because it crosses class, race, gender, age, and other lines to address us as members of a common group. It hails us as equals. To the extent that we all share in its discourses we share a common project.

Postmodern theories that posit endlessly decentered subjects and differentiated audiences and textual practices are clearly right about one level of cultural reality. Postmodern theory and the various cognitive and cultural tendencies it explains and describes are obviously (in my view) correct in pointing out strong social tendencies and their ramifications. But, like the other examples of difference theory I have mentioned, they mimic the very totalizing tendencies they claim to abhor by assuming difference and fragmentation are far more powerful and pervasive than they are, that they have assumed the position of cultural dominant in a way that does not allow for contradiction or even unevenness in development (see especially Collins 1989). This is overly generalized as a description of what our common world is really like. The fact is that, in spite of these obvious changes in our social and affective lives, we do all inhabit—perhaps in new and problematic manners—a common world that shares a common sense of reality at some level of our conscious existence. To say otherwise is to defy common sense. And to the extent that we do inhabit a common discursive, cultural environment, that environment is best represented by the kinds of television programming we all experience, especially those examples—and TV movies are among the most common of this category—that we tend to experience together, often as a majority of the television watching public.

Because I am taking this particular perspective on television's textual practices and audiences, I am going to be talking about raw content in ways that may seem to some readers theoretically naive (although I am always conscious of the fact that I am speaking in commonly understood, naive terms about social and psychological representation and my statements are based upon implicit theoretical formulations). My project is to analyze the ways in which textuality operates as a mode of dealing with actual social reality in the most direct political sense of mediating in the formulation of social belief and action, both private and, especially, collective and public. Therefore, I must naively discuss the (obviously naturalized and distorted) realist texts as they are understood and discussed in public discourse—as identifiable, shared versions of social and personal reality.

Introduction

In discussing texts, I will therefore slide past Bourdieu's distinction between "naive" and "aesthetic" readings that distinguish the distanced, self-conscious ways in which theorists and other intellectuals receive texts and the more naive reading practices that he describes as characterizing the working class (Bourdieu 1981, 4). Television is a popular cultural form addressed to a lowest-common-denominator popular audience. But it also works to address and engage those who participate in struggles over meaning from positions of greater differential strength. While we who have greater cultural capital may read differently, or at least in more complex ways, we are never totally distanced from the more common subject positions from which the rest of the public reads. Bourdieu's categories are themselves heuristic; they oversimplify the realities of reception with broad class distinctions. Obviously, we as intellectuals move up and back between naive and aesthetic stances.

I raise this issue because it explains my stance as an author, my way of dealing with the problematic of television realism and my own choice of writing style and voice. Except in this introduction, I will not refer to matters of textuality in great detail and will instead speak, very often, as though texts were more transparent than they obviously are. Although I will certainly "read" them structurally rather than realistically, I will use the language of bourgeois realism to do this. This is a tricky and not always possible task. It forces oversimplifications at times and certainly brackets off whole areas of textual complexity. On the other hand, the loss in theoretical subtlety is offset by the enormous gain in cultural accessibility. It allows for those with different levels of cultural capital to, I hope, enter a common discursive site.

In other words, I am writing across audiences. I am hailing my readers—intellectuals, media theorists, and TV fans—as a single audience defined by their involvement with television texts as both entertainment and discursive site for the negotiation of actual social and political problems. In the years since media theory has developed its current linguistic and stylistic practices, a wedge has been drawn between those who "study" and "analyze" and those who merely "watch" or "receive." Terms that are, like the professional languages used by doctors, lawyers, economists, and others, shorthand devices for conversation among an initiated elite, mostly students and scholars of certain prestigious academic departments, have been developed. This is understandable and serves many important functions.

From another point of view, however, it leads to the false and perhaps dangerous implication (it is rarely stated) that theorists do not have the same stake in the actual content of texts as others, that we who write books and journal articles are not also citizens with concerns and responsibilities. This, like so many of the post-structuralist turns in theory, leads to a situation in which theorists are not involved in the actual social world by virtue of the very sophistication and depth of what they know about "reality."

Roland Barthes addresses this issue in the final pages of *Mythologies*. "Any myth with some degree of generality . . . represents the very humanity of those who, having nothing, have borrowed it," he says. And "to decipher" these myths "is to cut oneself off from those who are entertained or warmed by them." And so, he goes on, "the mythologist is condemned to live in a theoretical sociality; . . . his connection with the world is of the order of sarcasm" (157).

In fact, for most of us, this is an exaggeration, to say the least. Or it ought to be. Among ourselves, we speak very much as anyone else does about movies, books, and television. Indeed, if we participate in more mainstream discourse—letters to the editor, op-ed articles, political speeches, television and radio talk shows—we drop this pose immediately. We do indeed, as citizens, as partisans of feminism, of affirmative action, whatever, intervene in popular discursive sites as though texts were more transparent than they are. We discuss characters and our immediate "nonaesthetic" responses to them in the same way as the most naive viewers. We have feelings about texts and characters that are linked to values and judgments. And we express them.

For a theorist to "fall" into this mode in a serious book is often considered illegitimate, a lapse into naïveté. But that is what I am knowingly doing here because I conceive of my audience as dual: I am addressing professionals and television viewers. I watch TV movies and have been affected by them; I have incorporated them into my private and political mediations with daily life. I take them seriously because of their engagements with social rela-

tions and issues of immediate import and because of their powerful ability to reach and move large segments of the public at large.

If TV movies exist in a public sphere that mediates between
viewers and their social and material existence, then so does this
book. The choice of what public sphere to enter to discuss popular culture and its power is not obvious. At what point does theory enter public discourse? At what point do we invite the audiences about whom we theorize to join the conversation? It
seems to me that if we take media seriously, we must want our
ideas to circulate outside the realm of theory, to be applied, as
math and economics are applied, to the real world.

I have chosen to write in a largely nonacademic style because
I want to engage the largest number of readers possible. I want to
be read by those who really watch and use TV movies and I want
to participate in directing the ways in which they may use them,
to point them toward a politicized view of themselves as citizens
and consumers of culture. This is tricky, although it is sometimes
done (Jenkins 1990, Lewis 1990). In the early days of feminist critique, when we still unself-consciously talked about ourselves as
members of the category "woman" it was done more often and
considered politically necessary. Today, especially in audience
and reception studies, we find the opposite tendency: a distancing of the writer from her ethnographic object of inquiry. There
are good reasons for this, of course. Bourdieu explains them
thoroughly in his taxonomy of cultural practices among various
social strata. Never losing sight of his teachings, however, I prefer
to navigate the sticky middle ground where television exists—the
public sphere—and to assume that certain theoretical matters are
understood. There is no other way to speak in raw political terms
about the stakes of these symbolic narratives, to reconnect them
to the lived social experience they affect.

Even if I were writing only for theorists, given my social and
political concerns here, I would have to avoid technical jargon
and excessively "textual" readings. First, they are distracting.
They too easily become an end in themselves, of interest (and
they are exceedingly interesting even as intellectual exercise) for
their own epistemological sake, operating as metalanguage inter-
rogating metalanguage. Often, the "problem" posed textually becomes, in one's mind, a problem solved fully in terms of textual

resolution. "Rather than set up an opposition between episodic series and the continuing serial along reactionary/radical lines," concludes an analysis of televisual narrative strategies, "I would prefer to view them as two different responses to television's dual ideological compulsions: the need to repeat and the need to contain" (Feuer 1986, 114).

Here we see how language and methodology serve to move us further and further from what is quite clearly a discussion of ideological matters, "reactionary" versus "radical" plot structures. And yet, because of the privileging of formal over substantive matters, the piece ends by moving far away from the connection—a felt connection for viewers—between what is happening to the people in the series and things in their own lives. We "know" that in series formats a binary opposition is at work textually. We know that one is called reactionary and one radical. But what are the issues? What are the stakes?

This particular piece happens to be analyzing Norman Lear's "All in the Family" series (a series that, like many of the TV movies I examine, was distinguished by its aggressive and blatant engagement with highly charged political issues). Like my TV movies, "All in the Family" engaged these issues through narratives that represented them as conflicts within nuclear families, families in which, as in TV movies, individuals embodied conflicting, contradictory social and moral characteristics and values that defined the terms through which ideological struggle was enjoined.

To read all of this textually reveals important truths about the way in which conventional narrative and realistic conventions serve to naturalize and contain radical change even as they allow progressive positions to enter the struggle. It is not sufficient to explain the intervention of such programming in actual social reality, however, because it leaves off at the point where broader public discourse—in the popular media and in the everyday social world—takes up, after the show has been aired.

Apart from the distraction of such detailed textual analysis, for the purposes of my own work, there is an epistemological issue here as well. It is well known that one's model, one's choice of discourse, determines what one is capable of asking and answering about an object studied. Donna Haraway addresses this issue in talking about the language used by defense analysts. She speaks of a 1987 article by Carol Cohn about participating in a seminar for strategic nuclear planners. Cohn "wrote about how enthralling and attractive it was," says Haraway, "how powerful you feel and how much fun it is to learn their language. And then you realize you've forgotten how to speak in other ways, that the questions you used to know how to ask can't be asked in this new language. You've forgotten how to translate and you've lost the pleasure of forcing the translation" (Haraway 1991, 75).

Haraway is referring, specifically, to the importance of connecting theory to social movements, of the impossibility of making the discourses of "apolitical" nuclear strategizing fit the ultimately political questions that discourses of social movement embody. "Without a social movement," she concludes, "I don't think it can be done" (75). I have the same concern about the kind of theoretical discourse I quoted above that translates political and social matters into textual ones in ways that make it impossible to incorporate the questions asked by socially conscious— much less activist—readers. Because of this I intend to use the language and "the questions" I/we used to know in the early days of cultural studies, when it was easier, in fact mandatory, to connect theory with Hall's "dirty world" out there.

Having said this much, I will sketch out my major theoretical assumptions about the textual practices of TV movies, trying to draw as full a picture of the cognitive map I travel as possible. Those concerning narrative and genre will be elaborated throughout the text.

First of all, I am addressing television texts primarily from the point of view of genre and narrative theory. TV movies, as a popular form, exist as an established genre with fixed structural components. Genre, as Jameson explains, exists as "a social contract" between an author and a society (1981, 106). It is a way of telling a collective story about issues we all agree are important to our common social well-being. Genre develops diachronically, retaining its structural bases but also being restructured and reenvisioned to fit changing historical and social realities and beliefs. Each new version asks us, "Do we still want to believe in this?" (Schatz 1981, 12–13). Does it still reflect enough of our sense of what reality is like, of what, ideally, it should be like?

Because genre is a collectively developed form, imbued with

the authority of something already consented to by its public and in fact inflected by the changes wrought by shifts in public experience and belief, its function is highly ideological. In fact, as Jameson further says, it is "essentially a socio-symbolic message . . . immanently and intrinsically an ideology in its own right" (1981, 141).

The TV movie is a genre that tells a story about the family. To the extent that it lends itself to progressive readings, it includes elements that work as a critique of the nuclear family, in terms of the genre's ability to provide the social and personal goods it is charged with providing in contemporary life. To the extent that it works to preserve dominant ideology, it does so by naturalizing those elements of family life that create unhappiness, insecurity, and pain, and by representing human suffering and discord as "essential" to human nature.

The genre is a discursive site upon which conflicts and contradictions inherent in the existence of the family as an institution within bourgeois society are worked out. Oppositional polarities between matters of privacy and political interventions, marital harmony and gender conflict, sexuality and maternity, economic values and those of love and nurturance, and similar issues are worked out within the context of a narrative pattern that is stable but maintains its stability by maintaining flexibility, by incorporating oppositional voices and concerns into an always shifting overview of what a "real" family is. It redefines the term *family* as much as necessary in order to maintain the myth that all personal problems in a capitalist society may be resolved by individuals who view themselves, essentially, as family members.

This conceit is in harmony with the televisual apparatus itself, which always interpellates its viewers as family members and as consumers of advertised commodities. It also works ideologically to set up a binary opposition between the "world out there" and the safe haven of the family "in here." Thus television positions us and addresses us as subjects whose concerns, as family members, are those of television itself. And this means that we are assumed to share the televisual assumption that "the family" is the source of all personal satisfaction and of all sense of political identity; that the world "out there" is engaged by us only in our roles as family members and that it is to be judged, and amended, in terms of its ability to fit family values. Advertising spokespersons and other voices of authority set up a relationship with the viewer that "creates complicity" in viewers by assuming "it has certain kinds of viewers and that it speaks for them and looks for them" (Ellis 1982, 164–65). It tells us how to negotiate the outside world, but always within the identity politics of families.

The world represented in TV movies mirrors the conditions of the family member subject positions constructed by this apparatus. The narrative works to resolve the conflicts and contradictions within families and between family values and those of capitalism in ways that the real world does not in fact allow. In other words, it works to preserve and reinforce the dominant family ideology, which falsely assumes a perfect harmony between these conflicting values.

The genre also works to neutralize all contradictory elements that cannot be reconciled to the dominant family ideology by excluding them from the constructed world in which the ideal families live or by naturalizing the causes of these problems so they seem fatally "tragic" rather than historical and political.

Thus genre is used as a means of negotiating contradiction and difference and maintaining dominance. But it works because it allows a far greater range of oppositional voices and experiences to enter the game and be legitimated. Its focus on such explicitly political and socially charged issues makes it a particularly powerful and significant form. Its figured modes of resolving the most vexing problems of our day gain authority and credibility because it partakes of lived reality in more complex, elaborated ways than other genres.

What John Fiske calls "real-seemingness," a sense of a text "being very much like" one's own experience, which is not dependent only on the strength of realist representational strategies but also on "the relevances . . . fans [are] able to construct between [the characters] as textual representations and their own everyday lives," the way fans can find in the behavior of characters "a way of articulating their own social experience" (Fiske 1990, 140), is pronounced in TV movies because of their richness of social and political detail.

Here is where the importance of the concept of preferred and oppositional readings comes in and how it fits into a view of television as a public sphere embodying public conversations and arguments. Let me elaborate, then, on some of the issues raised earlier about texts and audiences.

The practice of reading a movie like *The Burning Bed* is of course on one level infinitely private and inflected by audience differentiation. But on another level it partakes of collective, political significance for large numbers of demographically chosen viewers for whom it constructs a preferred address: women. "Cagney and Lacey" is another example of this. It is directed at a female audience assumed to have some sympathy for (implicit) feminist thinking. Fiske's student is not the only young woman to read "Cagney and Lacey" personally, as a "real-seeming" representation of her own social experience. If we bracket off the issue of difference in her situation and slide over it to include her in our heuristic category "woman," we can easily see that to the extent that she uses the text to articulate her position in the power relationships of her world, she shares that with other young women who have watched the show. Thus, her private reading of the text links her to others. It is intended to, for contradictory reasons. It means to address her as a member of her gender and to convince her that she and her sisters can be served within a social structure that cannot in fact fulfill this promise without substantive structural change.

This is not by accident. The producers of "Cagney and Lacey," like those of *The Burning Bed*, encoded the oppositional voices of feminists and other women quite intentionally. Julie D'Acci's study of "the ways in which several discourses and discursive practices . . . interact to produce the characters of Cagney and Lacey [and] construct a variety of interpretations of the characters" charts the intersections of various participants in the production process, including the press, certain audience members, and the television industry, among others (D'Acci 1987, 205). The oppositional voices, the polysemy of the text, owe at least some of their strands to the impact of already politicized women and to the idea of "feminism" circulating discursively during the time the show ran. In one sense, then, we can interpret the oppositional, or politicized, reading of Fiske's young woman as one end of a conversation between two generations of women, second-wave feminists and the young women who came after them. By viewing television as a public sphere, we can thus conceptually connect private interpretive practices to more potentially activist ones.

Another way in which TV movies serve to facilitate audiences' movement up and back between text and social reality is in their contextual operations. Since television is a heterogloss of discourses and voices, the narrative unity of the drama itself is always threatened by the shifts and fragmentations of the flow. In particular, the tendency of the networks to append news stories about the actual characters represented in the movie, or about others suffering from the same problems, works to distance viewers from the dramatic identification attempted through realism and to facilitate the making of connections between individual mythologized heroes and actual similarly situated groups of like individuals. In a Brechtian way, the pointing up of the fictional, symbolic nature of the "story," occurs when, for example, the actual Francine Hughes is pictured in the news follow-up to *The Burning Bed*.

On the other hand, the conservatizing effect of other kinds of texts—especially advertisements with their blatant propagandistic reinforcements of the status quo—is also part of the flow. News reports may counteract whatever credibility oppositional positions may gain in TV movies by presenting statistics denying the seriousness of problems or touting new medical or legal practices that are presumed to make the problem obsolete. In the babel of multivocality that forms the two-hour segment of television within which a TV movie is broadcast, all these things interact in contradictory ways. In what follows, all of this is implicit or explicit.

1

The American Dream Machine: Movies for Large and Small Screens

Before looking analytically at the various manifestations of the TV movie genre that is our subject, it is necessary to look at the history and institutional structure out of which it was born and through which it gradually took on the conventions and tensions that now characterize it. That is the purpose of this first, lengthy chapter. While in the body of the book I will look closely at the telefeature from a variety of critical perspectives, none of this makes much sense socially without a clear (if necessarily somewhat simplified) overview of the forces that produced it and the way it is now created out of a variety of complex, often contradictory forces and tendencies. If the TV movie matters, and I am certain it does, it matters in the context of such material only. It is both a social and a cultural form, and the fascinating interplay of the social and cultural makes study of the form rich and rewarding. It affects people but not only as drama. It is at least as much a function of its obvious role in the public arena—a role acknowledged and understood, if only unconsciously, by viewers of all kinds—that it compels. It is about something important. It comes to us via a variety of people who have power, who matter, who make things happen. When we get—at the end of this book—to the study of viewer experience and response, it will be a given, because of what we learn in this first chapter, that such experience and response are not merely personal, private, and subjective. They are social, public, and determined, at least partially, by political and economic intentions that are easy to locate and document at this early point of textual production.

The history of TV movies begins with the birth of theatrical films a hundred years ago and continues through the present time, when the dominant, most socially powerful form of dramatic narrative is produced for and aired over TV screens and not in movie theaters. Thus the similarities and differences between film and television, as technologies and as social and cultural forms, are key to a full understanding of what the movie has always meant in American society and what it now means. That its economic, institutional, and even physical and psychological situation is radically different in 1990 from what it was in 1890 is a function of the evolution of media forms in a dynamically changing social context.

Having spelled out the genealogy of the social issue feature film and analyzed its early determinants, I will look closely at the networks today, at how they operate, how their executives think, how the tensions between the various people in power, many of whom have different agendas and indeed operate out of different organizational structures and ideological orientations, do their daily work. How do they decide what movies to make? How do they smooth out the glaring differences in the needs of sponsors, network heads, and creative workers? How do they determine what will work and what will not, given their multilayered, often far from exact sense of what the effects of different decisions—about content, scheduling, commercial breaks, and so on—actually will be.

Once we have looked at this matter, in its own institutional (as opposed to theoretical) context—in other words, in its day-to-day, often vulgar concreteness—the generic and textual readings, which will of course refer back to this chapter, not only will make more sense but also will acquire another dimension, one informed with elements of lived reality that only this kind of concrete descriptive detail can provide.

Social Issue Drama: From MGM to NBC

The movies—most obviously theatricals, but now, more significantly than we may realize, TV movies too—have been the generators of mass social dreams from their inception in the 1890s. In

2

the two decades separating World War II from the Vietnam era, the mid-1940s to the 1960s, American life and culture underwent massive changes. So did the form, function, and medium of mass American dreams. The movie industry, in a state of anxiety and confusion over its internal health, did not in any sense die. In retrospect, we can see that it did not even swoon into the permanent, lingering decline so many were forecasting. By the end of the 1980s, certainly, it was enjoying boundless health and prosperity.

Nonetheless, the movie industry's social role and personality have been transformed over the last decades. Home television, which emerged into cultural prominence and, very soon, dominance in the 1950s, had a lot to do with this, although not as much as casual commentators often suggest. In fact, while squabbling and whining like a toddler faced with a new baby in the house, the movie industry, after many false starts, in time figured out a way to live accommodatingly with its new sibling.

This accommodation meant, however, that new turf boundaries had to be drawn. Theatrical films, which during the 1930s and 1940s were the major source of social issue dramas—many of which influenced the direction of public discourse on matters like race, religious prejudice, and war—increasingly, since the advent of television, have been geared toward blockbuster extravaganzas and youth-oriented films. It is, after all, kids—the dating crowd—who always want to get out of the house and socialize, particularly at the new suburban malls that have become the social centers of middle America (Rapping 1988, 14). Their parents, on the other hand, prefer to stay in, avoiding babysitter costs and parking problems, and watch current movies on their home TV screens, via cable or videocassette recorder. The need and desire for more meaty, challenging narratives that dramatically pose and resolve the central concerns of the nation at large remains.

If movies increasingly renounced this task, in part perhaps out of fear of competing unsuccessfully with the small, home-centered screen, it remained for television—which in news, talk shows, and magazine formats already played the role of arbiter of social issues, concerns, and values—with an open field to develop an adult movie form of its own, the made-for-TV movie. The telefeature, or movie of the week, came, most interestingly, to replace the Hollywood social issue film. Coming on the scene in 1964 and rapidly becoming established as an important economic and dramatic form by 1972, with the airing of *Brian's Song*, its first ratings blockbuster, the TV movie has, in less than twenty years, become the dominant mass form for the dramatic portrayal of major social issues.

Before looking at the TV movie and its differences from its precursor, it is necessary to examine the history of the American movie and its development from its original theatrical form to its television version. This is obviously not the place to do this in great depth, and it has in fact been done very well by others (see especially Sklar 1975). We are concerned here with the most central factors—social, economic, and cultural—that defined the formation of the two kinds of movies with the similarities and differences that their sometimes linked, sometimes very separate histories produced.

From Nickelodeon to Cineplex

Movies, "the first of the modern mass media" (Sklar 1975, 1), are unique in American culture. The reasons they were able to become so powerful a cultural form had much to do with their unusual social history. Unlike many earlier forms, movies never reflected the single vision of a dominant class. Rather, they were from their inception destined to be a form characterized by their ability to bring together and somehow arbitrate among the many conflicting visions of a huge and powerful nation filled with contrasts and contradictions. They served, through their larger-than-life yet generically simple and repetitive narratives, to create visions of the American Dream struggled for and ultimately achieved by a set of heroes and heroines—the royalty of an industry-created star system—with whom Americans could identify. Good and evil, success and failure, love and war—these terms came to be defined in large part by the celluloid fantasies experienced in the darkened movie houses of urban and small-town America. But these were not simple, one-dimensional terms. Rather, they held in fragile, always tenuous balance a mass of warring values and dreams.

As with all cultural phenomena, any real understanding must involve a sense of the interlocking influences of a variety of forces. Social history, business history, and the history of developing technologies all help explain the power of movies over the American imagination. Thomas Edison predicted that movies, along with his own phonographs, were destined to provide entertainment for the wealthy (Bordwell and Thompson 1986, 346–49). Because of the changes in the social and economic life of the times, this was not destined to be the case. On the contrary, the decades encompassing the turn of the century—the years in which movie technology and exhibition forms developed—were years of massive shifts in American population and city life. Industrialization, the rise of the machine as a means of mass production of commodities of all kinds, brought the triumph of consumerism as well as mass media. "Mass communication," as Stuart and Elizabeth Ewen have argued, is "not an isolated phenomenon of twentieth-century capitalism" but an integral aspect of industrialization as a whole. Because the move from home production to mass production and distribution of commodities for personal and home use also involved production of mechanical images, "channels of popular sensibility and desire" (Ewen and Ewen 1979, 16 and 27), in the form of advertising and popular culture, became linked inexorably with channels of production and marketing.

The influx of huge numbers of immigrants from Europe, as workers and as consumers, radically changed the urban landscape. Neighborhoods became ethnically and economically separate in ways never before experienced in American life. Different ethnic groups did not interact. They tended, even, to have separate art forms, for their experiences, desires, and needs were increasingly different. Silent films, shown first in nickelodeons and then in neighborhood movie houses, were suited to immigrant groups for several reasons. Most obviously, they were accessible to those who could not yet speak English. With their stories of love and life in the new country, they had enormous appeal to immigrants, themselves "caught up in the drama of social transformation" (Ewen and Ewen 1979, 81) in personal ways. At the movies, immigrants learned important lessons about how to be American. But they also learned a subtler message: to be American meant to nourish dreams of love, success, and lifestyles very different from those of the old country.

Movies thus entered the scene as working-class, low-brow entertainment and held little interest for the educated and wealthy. Far from being regarded as an art form, movies—like all new forms, from the penny novel to rock and roll—were considered a moral disgrace. Many of the early producers and theater owners were themselves of this immigrant working class (Sklar 1975, 25–31), a fact that made the form both more interesting as a social phenomenon and easier for the gatekeepers of high culture to dismiss. By the time movies rose to a position of general viewership and interest, their class and immigrant roots were firmly established.

But the rest of movie history shows a clear struggle for control of the visions and dreams that had captured American imaginations and hearts everywhere. As with every major industry, regulation came to the movie industry quickly in the form of a series of boards and agencies that set standards for production. The moral dictates of these groups, along with the needs and desires of the financial backers and those of the producers, who had to please and draw audiences, made for a complex and prolonged battle. But out of this battle, in which the conflicting needs of every group and class in the country played a part, came a cultural form far richer and yet more unruly than previous forms (Rapping 1983, 72–74). Movies became an arena for the working out of a general mythology that would reflect both dominant and alternative dreams and would, in fact, define the rules by which these contradictory elements—hope and restraint, progress and containment—would come to coexist.

The tensions and strains of this implicit struggle inform the major movie genres of the Golden Age—as they would, in a different form, inform the TV movie. In a sense, all major movie genres can be read as social issue genres because they all have, as underpinnings, the conflict and ultimate resolution of differing visions and values at war in the American social landscape. In the Western we see the utopian dream of freedom, of life in harmony with the vast natural landscape of the continent in conflict with encroaching industrialism and greed. In the romantic and musical comedies, we see, in romantic terms, the conflicts between classes and the happily-ever-after resolution of those conflicts in the marriage of a heroine and a hero of different backgrounds. "You say tomato and I say tomahto / Let's call the whole thing off" gives way to accommodation and the dream of a social world in which such differences and the prejudices that exacerbate them are overcome. In their place we get a melting-pot view of American life—a brave new world in which the American family itself melts into cultural and class love and bears new, tolerant fruit (Rapping 1983, 84).

Social realism, and the classic "social issue" film, had a particular place in American culture tied more visibly than the Western or musical, for example, to actual social tensions and crises of belief and harmony. The 1930s, a period of enormous change and upheaval, saw the birth of two film forms that dealt openly with social issues, the crime film and the women's film. That it is only the crime or gangster film that has traditionally been viewed as an obviously social manifestation of the depression is not surprising, given the tendency to dismiss all things feminine as trivial. Nonetheless, the women's film—described by one historian, as recently as 1978, as mere "escapist fare . . . embodied by teacup dramas and confession tales" (Earley 1978, 51)—clearly reflected as strongly as the film of the streets erupting tensions in American life. The two forms work together, actually, as the "male" and "female" versions of the stresses and tragedies of American social life. If the "male" genres dominated the theatrical film, set as it was in the public social space of the street, however, the telefeature, viewed in "female" domestic space, would have a different emphasis.

But, to move back to our brief film history, the depression was a period of great creative and economic growth. The advent of sound brought a new dimension. Less obviously, especially to the bankers who began to be far more cautious about investing in movies because people had less money to spend, the hard times produced a greater need than ever for entertainment, both as escape (a derisive term for the desire to invest more time in the utopian dreamwork of culture) and as a form of understanding and coming to terms with harsh social reality.

While the bankers have never been as interested in individual scripts as the sponsors of television drama later would be, they did begin to exercise stricter control over production, demanding more rigorously standardized offerings that could be efficiently produced and involve the least possible box office risk (Wasko 1982, 47–69). These dictates determined the conditions for the development of the studio and star systems and the corresponding development of a genre-oriented industry (as opposed to one that would have allowed *auteurs* to develop individual styles and visions).

This restriction on artistic creativity was offset, however, by the creative energies brought to film by the new writing talent hired to accommodate the move to sound. Now it was possible to produce far more sophisticated works, and by 1935 studios were bringing in well-known journalists and novelists to write scripts. These writers, many of whom came directly from the urban areas in which economic tensions and stresses were most dramatic, had a social perspective more finely developed than the studio heads were used to. So did the playwrights and novelists who came to Hollywood to work in the exciting new medium. The colony of writers in Hollywood in the thirties included Lillian Hellman, Dorothy Parker, Clifford Odets, Scott Fitzgerald, William Faulkner, and even, for a time, Ernest Hemingway. These were writers of strong left-leaning tendencies, filled with social and political passions that they attempted to place onscreen.

To some extent, they did. But there were always restrictions on what they could do and how they could do it. These restrictions came in part from financial and moral institutions, but a more interesting source of limits came from Hollywood itself. If the studios demanded somewhat simple, predictable genre films, there was also an increasing sense, in Hollywood, that the studios were in the business of creating more than profits or entertainments. The sense of self-conscious mythmaking came to the studios at a time when self-consciousness about American culture was in the intellectual air (Sklar 1975, 195–219). The studios took what they wanted from the new literature of American culture and, inevitably, twisted and turned its various, often conflicting, ingredients to handle an increasingly serious, downbeat subject matter in ways that would not seriously offend or subvert dominant institutions and beliefs.

The gangster film, filled with realistic images of what poverty breeds in an immigrant population brought up on visions of success, happiness, and rags-to-riches heroes and heroines, had various messages. One was, undoubtedly, that poverty breeds crime, that it is a "social problem" that a society committed to democracy and equality must eradicate. The other was, of course, that crime doesn't pay. The image of Jimmy Cagney yelling "Top of the world, Ma" only to tumble, bloody and defeated, to its bottom, is engraved in all our minds. So, if less often mentioned, is the image of Joan Crawford and her ambitious, driven sisters breaking domestic and sexual codes to rise from the streets to the mahogany rows of capitalist heaven, only to fall tragically and in isolation to their real or metaphoric deaths.

Through the late forties, Hollywood produced a certain number of socially conscious films about more specific issues. *The Grapes of Wrath*, about migrant workers, and *Gentleman's Agreement*, about anti-Semitism—to name only two—dealt seriously with issues of the day that called into question the promise of the American Dream and showed the tragic implications of its failed vision.

By the end of World War II, Hollywood was in serious trouble, as were its progressive tendencies. The coming of television, McCarthyism, and the Paramount antitrust decision of 1949, which ruled that vertically integrated studios could no longer maintain ownership of all three aspects of the industry—production, distribution, and exhibition—combined to send the industry into a tailspin of anxiety and confusion. Ideologically, the most obvious effect was the blacklist and the fears of political controversy and "subversion" it bred in the studio heads.

This was not the only reason for Hollywood's move to lighter, less demanding fare, however. Neither was the competition from television, which is generally seen as the single dominant cause of the cultural and economic decline of film (although the industry heads certainly saw it as such and took various measures to confront it). The truth is that television was only one aspect of a major transition in American work, home, and leisure patterns, a symptom rather than a cause of cultural change in America after the war.

It is certainly true that Americans moved in droves out of urban centers and into the suburbs, where movie theaters were not yet as numerous as in the old neighborhoods. It is also true that this new lifestyle, based on commuting and "bedroom communities" to which men returned late in the day, led to a tendency to stay home and watch television more, rather than going out to a movie or anywhere else. But even had we remained in cities, as many of us obviously did and always would, television's role in private life would have been critical. As Raymond Williams argues so convincingly in his groundbreaking 1975 study of the medium, television was brought into the marketplace, after the technology had been in place for three decades, when industrialism itself produced social conditions that demanded a home-centered system of communication, not just for entertainment but also for information—especially news and public announcements of every kind—and for advertising.

What Williams calls "mobile privatization," the lifestyle of a society in which large corporations demand mobile workers who will uproot themselves easily and settle in new, strange communities, made for a world of atomized, alienated people. Where we had, at least to some extent, maintained certain kinds of stable communities and extended family relationships throughout the first half of the rocky, unsettling twentieth century, by the 1950s it was apparent that this was no longer so. The family, actually in the process of "breaking down" throughout the rise of industrial capitalism, now appeared rather glaringly in its shocking disarray. So did the church, the educational system, and other traditional means of socialization and community integrity. Increasingly, the values of the marketplace replaced them as sources of national belief and value systems, and those in power, linked as ever to the kings of industry, saw home television as a way of congealing and controlling this new ideological system.

The Movie of the Week:
An Apparently Insignificant Birth

At this point the subject of TV movies—which did not appear until the sixties and did not actually become a cultural mainstay until the seventies—becomes relevant. For, over time, the TV movie replaced the Hollywood social issue feature. In fact, TV had bypassed every other institution in America as the disseminator of national myths and dreams.

Back in the movie studios in the late 1940s, few of the changes taking place in American life were obvious. The common wisdom that paints the movie moguls as prejudiced fools who refused to deal with their lowly upstart competitor has recently been exploded (Gomery 1983, 208–27). Far from ignoring television in anxiety-ridden paralysis, the studios saw immediately that they needed not only to negotiate with it, but also to buy into it. Their behavior indicates that they did, roughly, anticipate the wave of the future in which media forms, as they emerged, would be absorbed into what we now know as media conglomerates. Of course the conglomerate part did not occur to them in those still-innocent days before Time, Warner, and friends began gobbling up the globe. They were still reeling from the effects of the antitrust decision, which had kept them from controlling all of their own single-product industry.

Nonetheless, the studios bought shares of major television properties and tried to develop forms of subscription and large-screen theatrical television. Among the reasons they could never gain a foothold was the fact that they were already on shaky ground with the Federal Communications Commission (FCC) over trust issues and, as a single-product, Los Angeles-based industry, they lacked the community involvement and political clout to influence the regulatory agency. The FCC after all viewed television not merely or even primarily as entertainment, but rather as a government trust meant to fulfill certain social goals and serve certain "public interests."

In any event, the only arena in which the moguls were successful was in forming production companies that would produce television material. It was not until the mid-1950s that the major studios began to rent their own films to TV. Local stations, lacking the network programming that is now available, had long been airing movies supplied by foreign companies. Their films were all the studios had to hold onto, but finally, in the early 1950s, RKO, then owned by General Tire and Rubber, auctioned its pre-1948 stock to individual stations at a profit of $25 million (Gomery 1983, 212), and the other studios followed suit.

By 1964, TV acquisition of Hollywood movies, which had

11

grown from 300 in 1952 to more than 10,000 in 1964, had slowed to a trickle. While the networks had, during the fifties, aired Hollywood features only as "specials" (like the annual CBS airing of *The Wizard of Oz*, which began in 1956), by the early sixties they had begun regular weekly programs such as "Saturday Night at the Movies." Clearly, huge numbers of home viewers were choosing to watch full-length feature films rather than series. This meant high ratings and money in the bank. By the 1970s, there were ten overlapping "movie nights" on the networks. Unfortunately, however, the studio stock was nearly gone and the studio heads were not about to give the networks their best features, nor would they lower the price for films they were willing to send to television.

At that point, the networks made a major decision. Reasoning that they could save large sums of money (rental fees were high, production costs for TV movies relatively low) they decided to begin producing their own features. A secondary consideration was that these movies could serve as pilots for new series (as they still do today). The first TV movie was NBC's *See How They Run*, broadcast in October 1964. A crime-chase film involving three kids stalked by syndicate killers, it had an impressive cast including John Forsythe, Jane Wyatt (of "Father Knows Best" fame), Franchot Tone, Leslie Nielsen, and George Kennedy. So ordinary as to be wholly forgettable, it nonetheless did very well, as did other tentative network attempts to do it themselves in the later 1960s.

By 1972, when *Brian's Song* aired, TV movies were a popular mainstay. While the ratings available list only series figures rather than individual special features, making it impossible to be entirely sure whether the content of individual films affected ratings or not, the fact that these series as a whole did wonderfully well against by then strong competition is absolutely clear. It is surprising, for example, to see that as early as 1971–72 , when "All in the Family" was a strong first-place winner, "ABC Movie of the Week" ranked fifth and "The NBC Mystery Movie" fourteenth (Steinberg 1980, 172–73). By 1983–84, in the midst of the "Dallas" years, three movie-of-the-week series, "ABC Monday Night Movie," "ABC Sunday Night Movie," and "CBS Tuesday Night Movie," ranked twelfth, thirteenth, and twenty-fifth respectively (Brooks and Marsh 1985, 1040). By then, of course, features run outside of series, like *The Burning Bed*, were outdoing most entries from these series and had a life of their own as special events (*Variety* January 4–10, 1989, 40–49). In fact, when we add single-movie ratings to this survey—*Burning Bed* outranked any of the movie series—it is clear that movies, in their TV incarnation, quickly became one of the most widely shared phenomena of mass culture.

Jumping even further ahead of ourselves, to the 1988–89 season, we can see not only that telefeatures, at their most popular, have continued to rival and outdo regular series of all kinds as well as airings of major theatrical films, but also that they consistently treat more serious matters as well.

Looking at ratings and shares for the 1988–89 season (*TV Guide* July 8, 1989, 9–15), we see that the most popular series, "The Cosby Show," "Roseanne," "A Different World," "60 Minutes," and "Cheers," averaged ratings ranging between 25.5 and 21.441 percent and audience shares of 41 and 35 percent. The top ten made-for-TV movies, by contrast, did significantly better. Their ratings ranged from 27 to 22.9 percent with corresponding audience shares ranging from 42 to 36 percent. Even more strikingly, the top theatrical films aired on television that year scored ratings ranging between 20.3 and 17.4 percent with shares ranging from 32 to 26 percent.

What were these TV movies that audiences tended to select so much more frequently than either the competing series or theatricals? It is interesting to look at the subject matter of these movies compared to the theatricals that, while faring less well, occupy comparable slots in their category. The list of top-rated theatricals aired on television in the 1988–89 season began with *Top Gun*, *Beverly Hills Cop*, and *Romancing the Stone* and included *Sudden Impact*, *Raiders of the Lost Ark*, and *Back to the Future*. However entertaining such films may be, they are clearly light, escapist entertainment. Not a single one of them deals with any real issues and many are not even set in a real world, contemporary or otherwise.

Again, by contrast, the top-rated TV movies (whatever their contradictions or aesthetic limits) are undeniably centered on matters that concern us as members of contemporary American society. The list starts with *I Know My First Name Is Steven*, a highly sensational but gripping docudrama about a boy kidnapped and sexually abused for seven years before returning to a family with whom he can no longer live comfortably. Along with *The Case of the Hillside Strangler*, *The Karen Carpenter Story* (about anorexia), and *The Rescue of Jessica McClure*—a hot-off-the-headlines bit of sentiment and sensation that nonetheless treated a more real and serious matter than, say, *Romancing the Stone*—there were the two parts (ranking fifth and sixth respectively) of *The Women of Brewster Place*, based on Gloria Naylor's sad, serious, and strongly feminist novel about black women in an urban ghetto. While these titles certainly reveal high doses of sensation and pathos, they also show, often in the most sensational cases (most obviously in the first and last titles), a serious, if often flattened and superficial, concern with current social problems. Whatever one says of "The Cosby Show" or "Roseanne," one can hardly say that. "Cosby" may show positive role models of black middle-class life, but it is not "All in the Family." It never treats issues of racism, sexism, homophobia, or poverty, as "All in the Family" did and as *The Women of Brewster Place* most definitely did.

Having so digressed, let us move back to 1964, a time when the longevity and impact of the TV movie could not have been predicted. The networks took a shot at the form because they needed movies and wanted to save money. As it turned out, the profits were far greater than anticipated and the ratings beyond anyone's expectations. Producing a typical TV movie cost only $750,000—no more than airing a theatrical. What is more interesting from our perspective, however, is the content of the best-running movies, even back then. A look at *Variety*'s list of all-time televised movie hits—which includes theatricals and telefeatures—is revealing. While *Gone with the Wind* continues to place in the top two slots, the top-fifty list includes a significant number of telefeatures. *The Day After* ranks third, *The Burning Bed* twentieth; *A Case of Rape* is number thirty-two, and *Brian's Song* still comes in at thirty-seven. These are all films with serious social and dramatic content, far more so than many of the theatricals—*Jaws, The Poseidon Adventure, Airport, Love Story*—that are listed alongside them.

What is even more interesting is, over time, the surprising number of the highest ranking telefeatures (according to *Variety*'s figures, which include reruns) that treat the most serious, downbeat subjects. *A Case of Rape*, about a woman who loses her husband, her reputation, and her case when she brings charges against an acquaintance who raped her, was shown in 1974, a full year before Susan Brownmiller's *Against Our Will* was published, heralding the start of the widespread public concern about the issue. This remarkable film still ranks thirty-second among all theatrical and telefeatures aired on television, and I am often amazed at the number of my students who have seen it and remember it, a number far greater than those who have read, or even heard of, Brownmiller's book. When I suggest that they read *Against Our Will*, many do.

Continuing our survey, we see that the movie ranking fifty-third, *The Feminist and the Fuzz*, was shown way back in 1971, at the very beginning of the rise of the TV movie, and before *Brian's Song*. While it was a traditional romantic comedy involving social opposites attracting, squabbling, and finally living happily ever after, its title illustrates the differences between theatrical and TV versions of this genre. Where the thirties-variety romance focused on class, but not in any way that was obviously spelled out, this one centers on sexual politics—spelled out in clear ideological terms.

In the earliest years of TV movies, of course, the biggest hits were far more sensational than this pre-"Cagney and Lacey" Sharon Gless vehicle. *Little Ladies of the Night, The Dallas Cowboy Cheerleaders, Dawn: Portrait of a Teenage Runaway*, and *Sarah T.: Portrait of a Teenage Alcoholic*, all shown in the 1970s, are still in the top 100. While they sound titillating (and obviously drew large audiences partly on that basis), they are actually—especially the teen-problem movies—surprisingly serious, almost documentary treatments of social and family issues. Viewing them alongside recent hits like *Something about Amelia* during weeks spent at the Library of Congress viewing rooms, I was startled at how well they held up as domestic drama and how somber, even preachy, was their educational, uplifting tone.

15

TV Movies from the Business Angle

Before going on to a discussion of TV movies as art or cultural form, perhaps we should detour back to Hollywood and take a look at how they fit into the overall scheme of network programming—what Nick Browne has called "the supertext," or the grand plan of network scheduling for a given season (Browne 1984, 585–99), which the total nightly programming of all three networks, taken together, represents. While much has changed about television and its production of telefeatures, some things have remained more or less the same. The economic reasons for producing TV movies, the dramatic, thematic, and narrative forms they take, and their place in the overall social/cultural role played by home television remain largely the same as in 1964, if some of the figures and techniques are radically different.

First, let us consider the FCC and its role in structuring and overseeing networks and affiliates. A station's FCC license requires that it air a certain amount of "public service" programming—which generally means news, documentaries, and other such socially informative and educational matter. Since television is a public trust that uses a national resource, the airwaves, to communicate, it is clearly responsible to government and taxpayers. Indeed, the FCC in some sense codifies what media scholar Raymond Williams suggests has always been government's intention as far as the development of home TV was concerned: it insists that community and national concerns be given time for the greater public good.

While TV movies were not originally seen as a part of this commitment to FCC mandates, but only as money makers, over the years the networks began to see them differently. As we have seen, social issue movies quickly garnered popular approval. With money as a bottom line, the executives could readily see how their own interest as capitalists would dovetail neatly with their need to serve the people.

There is yet another twist to this grand scheme. The FCC also requires that local stations be free to run material that has direct bearing on local concerns. If this mandate were taken seriously, we would have much less national programming of all kinds—including telefeatures about current national concerns—and much more locally produced and oriented fare, but this Jeffersonian ideal of decentralized communities with distinct cultures and structures rarely is realized. Except for the highly lucrative local news, affiliates rarely produce their own programs. It is more profitable for them to accept network programs, for which they are given "station compensation." The only time affiliates actually balk at network fare is when programming is deemed potentially controversial and likely to turn away viewers.

While this kind of caution has traditionally been seen primarily in highly religious, conservative, or rural areas, in recent years it is far more common everywhere. This is because of the growing power (or what appears to executives as the probable power) of conservative lobbyists like the "moral majority" with their threatened boycotts of morally or politically "liberal" programs.

So now, added to the networks, sponsors, and FCC, we have public interest groups joining the battle over what will be seen on television. In fact, it is not only the right that brings pressure to bear on networks. Feminists, gays, and other more progressive groups have obviously had a significant impact on programming. Networks usually do not cancel controversial shows, and sometimes they run them at a loss when sponsors bolt. This has happened in such cases as *The Women's Room*, *Roe v. Wade*, and *The Day After* (which was not controversial politically but nonetheless made sponsors nervous about being associated with a film that portrayed the nuclear destruction of the world).

If networks do not automatically cancel controversial programs, even when affiliates are queasy or rebellious, they do analyze the costs and benefits of airing those programs. Matters of image and public opinion vie against dollars, for even a controversial show—in fact, very often a controversial show—may gain huge ratings in the vast majority of markets that air them. Losses in immediate sponsor revenues are then weighed against future earnings based on the higher advertising rates high ratings will earn later.

It is clear that the number of factors and the number of groups that contribute in various ways to the complicated process of determining what gets on television are very large indeed. Moreover, the motives and goals of any particular group or individual may be a strange mix.

How do the networks try to make sense of it all, and what are their central operating principles? The work of Todd Gitlin in *Inside Prime Time*, a chronicle of the daily operations of the network based on a few years of close observation and interviews, is invaluable in answering these questions. Later, we will look more closely at Gitlin's methods and at some of the possible biases and omissions that make his treatment of TV movies among the weakest aspects of his study. At this point, however, his raw data is, and has remained, the best information we have, primarily because of his close and deep textual constructions of processes and conversations (Gitlin 1984, 165).

Of particular interest here is his description of how the networks try to gauge what the traffic will bear politically and morally. These judgments tend to be hunches based on observations of life in Beverly Hills and information from the print media—*Time* and *Newsweek*, for example—that most resemble their own news shows. To the extent that television itself is a major contributor to the *production* of public sentiment, such hunches, when acted upon, reinforce what TV people believe to be the mood of the time. During the Vietnam War, for instance, Norman Lear developed a string of liberal sitcoms based on his and his bosses' shared hunch that people would be sympathetic. Today of course we have much more conservative views of family life because producers and executives sense that is the tenor of the times.

While this description is true as far as it goes, it is obvious that political, not to mention cultural, life is far more complex than this. It is also obvious that with all the actors involved in the drama, tensions and conflicts will emerge within the supertext as well as within individual shows. Even without the factor of creative energy and vision (a factor too often dismissed by media analysts in their fervor to paint a totally deterministic and philistine picture of network programming) there are the many complications and doubts that go with satisfying a multifaceted master. In any given season there are obviously programs, on each network, with radically different (or at least as radically different as the system permits) stances. Even the most groveling, unimaginative producer must wonder what to do about certain subjects for which no verdict is in or how to interpret the political meaning of a certain script. Moreover, the number of interest groups whose influence is considered strong enough to warrant concern is always large, and their concerns cannot all match. I could go on, but we will see this confusion at work in the next chapter.

Until then, it is safe to say that in the realm of TV genres, the telefeature is at any given time the most suitable form for dealing thoroughly not only with complex social issues but also—as we will see—with the most resonant of tensions, contradictions, and ambiguities. In the planning stages, however, it is also the most likely to get in the crossfire of political forces. Unlike the news, for instance, its claim to truth and historical incontrovertibility always appears to be a bit shaky. Moreover, it is a hybrid form, part fact and part fiction, part information and part drama. The rules of ideology, if they were as clear as some critics seem to assume, would be difficult to impose upon a form whose lifeblood is, no matter how superficially, such aspects of dramatic narrative as plot, characterization, atmosphere, and a mass of tensions and conflicts among and between all of these. In other words, when a drama "works" emotionally—which is a function of a combination of factors that cannot be anticipated or controlled entirely at the business end—it is in great part because of the talents, visions, and interactions of writers, directors, producers, and actors. Formula or no, money motive or no, this cannot be gainsaid. Joanne Woodward is to some extent the same artist on stage, screen, or video.

Actually, it is the producer rather than the director who gives form and life to the TV movie. The networks today do not produce their own feature films but contract to have them done by independent producers. These producers must pitch ideas to executives in competition for a limited number of slots during any season, and they must keep money and ideology very much in the foreground at this crucial stage: they depend on network financing because they cannot afford to produce films alone. The networks, for their part, insist on various certainties. They require specific writers, directors, and, especially, stars before they sign a contract. And they demand control of money—which determines schedule, production values, and quality of the other technical and artistic crew members (who, though invisible to the public, are as important technically to the final product as anyone else and who, in sheer numbers, actually dominate the process).

The networks themselves of course are funded by sponsors who pay for the right to run commercials on specific shows or at specific times. The affiliates accept this national advertising for a fee paid and the right to run local ads at certain times during the slot. In the early days it was common for sponsors to own shows outright and so to exert direct control over content. In the 1960s, the networks began to exert more and more control, and most shows were then licensed to networks, which sold time slots to sponsors. At that time there was also a shift to "spot advertising": sponsors bought advertising slots on specific shows rather than sponsoring an entire program. The higher the ratings for that show, the more the networks could charge for advertising time.

By 1970, when the telefeature was coming into its own, the ratings system had undergone massive changes. Before that, ratings had measured only gross numbers of viewers for given shows. In the late 1960s, however, marketing research came to television. NBC researcher Paul Klein, who later became vice president in charge of "audience measurement," was responsible for two innovations. First, he noticed that rather than watching particular programs, people simply watch television as a flow of fragments over a time span. From this observation he developed the idea of least objectionable programming: since people simply watch what they have on, it is more profitable to discover what the most people find unobjectionable enough not to turn off than to try to provide what they actually want to watch.

His other innovation was demographic, the study of which segments of the population viewed particular programming. If it turned out (as it did) that, say, affluent, heavy-spending segments of the country watched a show that, in the aggregate, had relatively few viewers, the show would stand a better chance of being retained because the sponsors of appropriate products stood to earn substantial profits. In this way, subtle judgments made on the basis of such factors as age, race, sex, geographic region, and so on came to inform the previously heavy-handed ratings business.

While Klein's two ideas are in some ways contradictory, they share a common focus: they rationalize decisions about money for the profit-oriented TV business. Entire network departments were formed to find formulas to make money by these methods. The materialism of this way of thinking needs no comment. We will return to the ratings system and view it from a different perspective later in this chapter. But first, let us take a look at the way in which telefeatures fit into network thinking and planning.

The Movie of the Week in Embryo

Television, at its birth, owed little to cinema. Its direct precursor was obviously radio: thirty- and sixty-minute time slots for news and series programs, with time for commercial breaks. TV news followed its radio model at least until the 1960s. Before the minicam came on the scene, there was little film footage; newscasters read from scripts while still shots appeared behind them.

TV drama also imitated radio, not film. Many sitcoms and other series came directly from radio. Sponsors' needs were felt, and since in these shows visuals were the major feature, the fit between ads and programs was unquestioned. Sets, clothing, and other details had to reflect the values and tastes portrayed in commercial messages selling commodities (Barnouw 1978, 106). The view of family life, of good and evil, right and wrong, by and large reflected the views of consumer capitalism.

Theatrical films obviously operate differently. For one thing, the "sponsor" is not visible, and the ties between funders and programs is less direct. Aesthetically, there are obvious and major differences. Movies are capable of pulling viewers into their imaginative universes by virtue of setting and technological sophistication and power. One sits in a darkened theater and watches larger-than-life figures and settings in images that are strong, bright, and detailed (Ellis 1982, 21–91).

TV, by contrast, is seen in a usually bright living room in which people move about, speak, and allow their attention to wander. The image is small and aesthetically inferior to film. Most importantly for this chapter, television, unlike film, must be written around commercial breaks in a series of brief scenes. The narrative must be clear and easy to follow in order to attract the largest number of viewers and hold their attention through commercial breaks, varying viewing times and patterns, and the competition of other channels (Ellis 1982, 173–94). For these reasons, television writers follow fairly specific writing formulas. Action is circumscribed, physically and intellectually, to fit the limits of video technology and the realities of home viewing.

We must consider all of this when we examine the actual mechanics of producing telefeatures. Obviously, when the networks began this venture, they were taking an old form, the "movie," and translating it to a medium for which it was not suited. Theatrical films had been shown on the small screen, and the problems were clear: the annoyance of commercials, the poor visual image, and the difficulty of following complex or subtle narratives, not to mention those that moved more slowly than the action series on the next channel. It was already obvious that the most positively received films were the simplest, in every way.

When they began to produce their own movies, the networks successfully rationalized the process in the interests of time, costs, and viewer acceptance. Writers learned to fit material to the medium's aesthetic and commercial needs. TV movies are generally broken into segments. The earliest segments are the longest, to capture viewer interest. Once viewers are hooked, commercial breaks are more frequent. Each segment is tightly constructed of actions and dialogue that further plot and do not confuse the viewer.

While the form of the genre has changed some over the years, as have the style and presentational devices, there is much more that has stayed the same. Even the political vicissitudes that accompany changing times are less apparent, or at least more ambiguous and varied, on the long form than in series television. This is clear from recent seasons. The Reagan/Bush years undoubtedly changed the slant of series TV. Even the most "liberal" family sitcoms—"Family Ties," for instance—are woefully lacking in substance or challenge to the right-wing vision of a stable nuclear family. There is far less difference between that show, spawned out of the experiences of 1960s activists raising children, and "The Cosby Show," which unblushingly mimics the self-satisfied conservatism of the 1950s models all these programs must to some extent follow.

Not so telefeatures. In 1989, along with heavily ideological films like *Adam*, about a father's brave efforts to find his missing son (among a list of some ten or eleven telefeatures of that season that focus on missing or otherwise endangered small children and feature strong male figures as patriarchal heroes keeping the traditional family intact and secure), such clearly antipatriarchal, feminist films as *Roe v. Wade* and *Brewster Place* also figured prominently. This may be what is most interesting about the form. Because the TV movie is shown only once (except for possible reruns) it takes more risks. It is not a staple of weekly scheduling, so it can be a bit adventurous. In fact, in many ways, that is its role on network television. It offers the spice (to use Gitlin's term) in a repetitive, static schedule, and that spice can be anything unusual or notable—including dissent from the network's political norm. Indeed, the reason the networks began to produce these features was, according to Gitlin, to "spice up the weekly schedule" (Gitlin 1984, 157). "The three networks now underwrite more original movies than all the studios combined," and TV movies take up a full 25 percent of prime time slots (Gitlin 1984, 168).

One of the most interesting ways in which TV movies have most obviously taken over the role of movies in the old studio system is in their mode of production. The network movies and miniseries departments have taken over where the studios left off at the end of the war, mass producing large numbers of feature films each year based on clear, simple guidelines and budget constraints, and using a more or less constant crew of workers from within the networks or in the crews brought together by the independent producers out of a stable list of preferred artists and technicians. Theatricals are now geared to packaged superstar blockbusters, but telefeatures, like the old studio films, are low-budget, formula narratives with brief lifespans. The average telefeature may cost $3 million or $4 million, the theatrical at least $25 million and usually more.

The money these films make, and the chance they offer to develop more complex stories and themes than series, make them attractive to the independent producers. About fifty producers, mostly in Los Angeles, pitch to networks regularly. They have a certain amount of artistic leeway: because a TV movie is shown only once, it can be more downbeat, even ending on a tragic note as a series cannot. Principals can be killed off without killing the entire season. The blacker sides of human nature can be explored without worrying sponsors or audiences too much.

As Lawrence Schiller, who produced the TV version of Norman Mailer's *The Executioner's Song* (a film so artistically excellent it played in first-run theaters in Europe) about Gary Gilmore, the convicted murderer who insisted on being executed, put it, "TV isn't afraid of downbeat stories because it doesn't depend on word of mouth" (Farber 1983, 46). In fact, TV movies are promoted entirely through promotional clips aired on the network itself. Like commercials, they demand attention by intruding within the regularly programmed fare. Also like commercials, they tend to be visually intense; in a few ten-second scenes, they play to the audience's love of sensation and drama. High concept is the word in the production of these teasers. "If you can't put the idea into a sexy sentence when pitching it," says Robert Greenwald, producer of *The Burning Bed, The Cheryl Pierson Story, Lois Gibbs and the Love Canal*, and other serious social dramas, "you can't sell it" (Greenwald 1985, 6).

Greenwald, always concerned with serious drama but also savvy about the system, found that one way to produce grim themes is to use top stars. His idea of casting Farrah Fawcett as the battered wife in *The Burning Bed* when she was known only for the jiggly "Charlie's Angels," while at first fought by the studios, turned out to be box office magic. The movie's success made Greenwald one of the hottest producers in town. Such are the contradictions of the form: feminism and seriousness are sold through sex and violence.

I do not want to overstate the seriousness of the form. Most TV movies are not *The Burning Bed*. In fact, networks would much prefer to play it safe with the TV equivalent of *Jaws*. "*Jaws* is a perfect television movie," says Deanne Barkley, the executive in charge of putting together telefeature deals at NBC, because "it can be summed up in a television log line" and "audiences know what they're coming to" (Gitlin 1984, 163). "It doesn't matter if they're good or bad," Barkley adds, perhaps superfluously. In fact, according to Gitlin, "executives came to regard the success of *Roots* and *Holocaust* as flukes" and concluded that they showed "anything might work once" (Gitlin 1984, 164).

Even in the "flukish" *Roots* and *Holocaust*, of course, the material was manipulated to fit the needs of the form and the network executives' correct or incorrect assessments of what audiences want. It is even more interesting to ponder the thinking of those executives who considered the high ratings for the most serious miniseries flukes. Obviously, they refused to consider the possibility that ratings would follow if they added more such programs. Instead, they continued to push their luck with a mishmash of serious and trivial features, looking for the perfect formula for how many, when, and what kind. It is as much for prestige and to meet FCC pressures to be "relevant" that they address social issues. Still, whatever their blind spot about the appeal of serious programming, appeal it does, perhaps for reasons beyond bottom-line thinking.

What we see in Gitlin's sometimes uninflected, sometimes (as I will analyze later) ideologically slanted descriptions of network executives' thoughts and actions has an interesting subtext. They make decisions and analyze results on the basis of assumptions that are not necessarily true. Why assume that the success of *Roots* was a fluke? Why not assume the opposite—that this unusual series, albeit for contradictory reasons (sex and violence vs. racial injustice, for example), spoke to a real hunger for knowledge and understanding of a painful, shared history that the mass media had not addressed this bluntly, if at all? If they made this alternate assumption, they would eagerly develop more and more such vehicles, until the market would hold no more, very much as they now develop endless clones of "The Cosby Show" until that particular take on that particular genre saturates audience attention. We will ponder these questions shortly. For now, we need to look more closely at the various attitudes and actions of the movers and shakers who confided in Gitlin.

Ads and their messages also color executives' thinking. Barkley, while never consciously considering the fit between ads and narratives, actually develops her ideas, at times, on the basis of well-known commercials because she sees them as "leads to trends" (Gitlin 1984, 168). AT & T's "reach out and touch" ads, for example, hinted that audiences would soon turn to old-fashioned themes of family and reconciliation. And so, while executives dismiss the ratings as guides to future hits when they seem to oppose the commercial wisdom, they do not, it seems, dismiss the less quantitatively verifiable popularity of *commercials* as indicators of what people want. Like many critics, the educated, upper-middle-class, wealthy people who run TV seem to believe the worst about their viewers' minds and desires.

In the end, then, we are left with certain questions about why and what people watch and who TV affects and how. Executives and critics alike have blind spots based on biases. And the raw data are too complicated and difficult to grasp and dissect to yield certain answers. We can only dig deeper and try to shape as clear an image as possible. Whatever the ultimate answers are, media analysts are not ready to state them now. As we shall see in the next chapter, while the creative staffs must follow the plans and schemes of the networks, they twist them a bit—or more than a bit—so that the results are somewhat different from the plans. As for what is experienced by viewers, that is an even trickier, more mysterious matter. On some level, one must admit that the work takes on a certain life of its own, as do all cultural products, and eludes analyst and accountant alike.

Methodologies, Meanings, and the Family-defined Spectator

The very issue of ratings needs some scrutiny. What are they? What do they measure? Do they work? What, really, are we saying when we quote *Variety* about ratings and shares of a 1970s movie like *The Feminist and the Fuzz* and one like *The Women of Brewster Place*, which was run nearly twenty years later under very different industry and social conditions?

It is a truism in the industry that the networks are not selling programs to audiences—they are selling audiences to sponsors. There is hardly a study of television that does not mention this. Network television, which is "free," makes its profit from sponsors who pay to place their ads in given time slots that are shown by the Nielsen ratings, which are television's way of figuring out who watches what, to draw a certain number of viewers. Ratings determine advertising rates and they are, as Todd Gitlin says, an industry "obsession" (Gitlin 1984, 51).

This system raises a number of questions. One is relatively simple: are ratings worth their position in industry thinking? A trickier question has to do with how the ratings are interpreted, what they are thought to mean. While there are several reasons to be skeptical about the accuracy of the figures, I tend to agree with Gitlin, a sociologist, that they are as reliable as they need to be in telling us, almost immediately at the end of the prime time evening, what people are watching (Gitlin 1984, 47). The major reasons for concern are probably, as Gitlin suggests, based on class and race bias. Nielsen workers may be reluctant to go into poor and black communities, so their figures reflect a heavily white audience and discount viewing habits of the huge poor and minority audience.

On the other hand, for industry purposes—at first implicitly and by 1970 quite specifically—the point of the studies is not to measure just any viewers, but rather those with the most expendable cash to buy sponsors' products. By the seventies, with the advent of demographic studies that actually broke down audiences into sectors based on age, class, sex and geographic location, this bias toward the wealthy was written as law. Demographic data come into play quite obviously in a study like this book, which assumes, for one thing, that women—the primary shoppers—actually do watch TV movies, and dramatic narrative in general, more than men do. In fact, in 1988–89, when I was preparing the proposal for this book, I read three Nielsen publications carefully. The first was the standard *1988 Report on Television*, which summarizes yearly figures on who is watching what, when, and where. Graphs illustrate how viewing choices have expanded and TV households have increased over the TV year. It lists viewing peaks, total number of household members, geographic location type, and variations in viewing by household characteristics and describes how households do their viewing by age, sex, race, and time.

This handy little pamphlet, along with others, *Total Women/ Working Women Viewing Study* and the very detailed *Perspective on Working Women* and their viewing habits by local markets, give clear information about what women want from television, at least given their options. It is unambiguously clear that—given their choice, which they did not always get (see Morley 1987)—women prefer family and romantic drama. This is important information, especially in light of the fact that we know how much sponsors and network executives rely on these figures.

My original plan was to discuss *only* specifically women-oriented TV movies. I decided to address the form in general, in spite of the obvious and intriguing "feminine factor," because it was far more difficult to dismiss the rest of the genre. Unlike romances and soaps, TV movies, like novels and theatricals, have many subgenres, of which the women's movie, while dominant, is far from definitive. Nor is it clear that the audience is all female. Men and children often watch "whatever is on" or "whatever Mom is watching." Families and television sets are very different from readers and books, and daytime is very different from prime time.

This ambiguity in defining audience also affects network thinking and decisions. Ideally, of course, a scheduler hopes for a perfect Platonic supertext in which each slot each night reaches an optimum number of viewers. But this is nearly impossible. It involves juggling so many unknown quantities, especially the relative importance—in terms of competition—of the other networks' choices. One of the network executives in charge of scheduling programs quoted by Gitlin says that he tends to ignore all the detailed information about who is watching what and when because it is actually too precise and detailed to be practical. Schedule juggling, which in the colorful parlance of Los Angeles he calls "playing with yourself," is in the end largely wasteful. It is a hopeless job. If, for example, a study shows a given program drawing four women, two youths, and one older man and another shows three youths, two women, and a man, what does it tell you? The fact is that audiences overlap during prime time and that conflicts among all the factors—lead-in versus lead-out power, competition with the other two networks' parallel programming (not to mention independents like Fox), and so on—are impossible to coordinate perfectly, even assuming you had the necessary product and, most crucially, you knew it would draw predicted numbers (Gitlin 1984, 60).

The second aspect of the ratings discussion is the question of what is measured by "the numbers." There is no question that, for industry purposes, at least in those departments concerned with numbers and profits, knowing the number of relatively awake and sober heads in front of a given image is money in the bank. Many executives devote all their time to this bottom-line is-sue. Many analysts also stress its importance as a way of correcting the more visible and perhaps popular impression that television is a form of communication and not a business, all text and no commodity. This is obviously a crucial point that viewers need to understand. It is also important that we all understand the most crassly materialist strategies and beliefs that govern much net-work strategy. In the early 1970s, when, as Ron Powers puts it in his discussion of the marketing of news, "TV news became too important to be left to the newspeople" (1977, 53) and marketing strategists were brought in from Madison Avenue to figure out how to program news, and later everything else, to achieve the largest possible audiences, demographics and concepts like least objectionable programming gained more control over the minds and budgets of network heads than perhaps was sensible or—certainly—healthy. Whatever the theoretical or ideological foun-dation of this hegemonic way of thinking, there is no way to deny its power or the results of its reign.

But the theorists and bosses may well be wrong about any num-ber of the balls they must keep in the air as they calculate, al-though there is too rarely a sense of that possibility in the things they say and do. In fact, there sometimes seems to be a sense of deep satisfaction on the part of intellectuals—in and out of the industry—in pointing out this bottom-line mentality and thus dis-missing all television "product" as junk. In Gitlin's interviews with the people who make television, this cynicism is a constant. Again and again they repeat a tragic refrain: I came to Hollywood to produce great art and these guys won't let me because it won't sell, because the cretins out there don't want it. Those rare mo-ments when they manage to achieve something they are proud of—"Hill Street Blues" comes up a lot in this context—are seen as flukes. "I got away with it," they seem to be saying, like so many schoolkids copying each others' homework.

There is much truth in this Baudrillardian sense of cynical resig-nation in the face of the totalizing visions of the wholly commodi-fied sign. I challenge it only because it has now become so widely assumed that it needs to be corrected and, for the purposes of this analysis, it leads to a certain kind of myopia that misses much of what is interesting on television and also demeans the average viewer.

Gitlin himself, in writing about the telefeature, is glaringly guilty of this ultimately class- and sex-biased tendency. "These B movies," he says of the telefeature, "come and go, leaving who knows what traces in the consciousness of our time" (Gitlin 1984, 157). And yet, while this sentiment is certainly generally true (as true as it would be for any TV genre), if one reads Gitlin closely, one discovers a funny slant to his thinking and a bias of his own— which resembles that of his informants—about what is "good." The only telefeature he treats with the same respect he gives middle-brow, male-oriented shows like "Hill Street" (the 1970s precursor of the 1980s *haute* yuppie series "L. A. Law" and "thirtysomething") is one that features a male hero. This movie, *Bitter Harvest*, is about a farmer who discovers that his cows are dying because of PBB poisoning and fights back against the government-sponsored use of this chemical. Gitlin uses this movie as an example of rampant self-censorship in the networks. The conventions of the form are often used as excuses to cut out political content. "Television drama abhors what it considers 'polemic, didactic,' " he says (Gitlin 1984, 175), and it insists on human-interest stories of limited scope that focus on individual, personal struggles and triumphs: thus the deletion at production time of a single line in this movie that said the hero's problem was "not an isolated case" (Gitlin 1984, 174). To say that, Gitlin argues rightly, would be to acknowledge that pesticide poisoning is actually a national, politically solvable problem and not a matter of individual strength and courage.

But his singling out of this movie and dismissal of most others is nothing more than sheer sexism. A much better political treatment of toxic poisoning and government and corporate complicity, *Lois Gibbs and the Love Canal*, aired at more or less the same time, is dismissed by Gitlin in a footnote. Moreover, its producer, the same Robert Greenwald who did *The Burning Bed* and at least fifteen other serious social issue dramas, many of which won Emmys and most of which were politically and dramatically notable and moving, is described offhandedly as having "a track record" based on such early "get into the game" works as *Portrait of an Escort* and *Portrait of a Centerfold*. Gitlin also ignores

Greenwald's *Lady Truckers*, although it is a funny feminist buddy movie about two women who steal a vicious trucker's vehicle and do all sorts of wonderful things while running from the police for a crime they did not commit—a surprisingly interesting little piece for the 1970s.

Greenwald is not only among the most serious craftsmen I have interviewed, he is also a committed progressive filmmaker. He came to Hollywood from off-off-Broadway to make television drama because he wanted to reach a large audience, and he studied the system carefully to figure out how to do it.

There is no reason I can think of other than a blind spot about women's issues and the female audience to dismiss Greenwald's considerable body of work so smugly while giving such a detailed account of a single, no more impressive (actually less interesting since it does not portray a working-class woman as heroine, as Greenwald's work generally does) movie by an unnamed director.

I am ending this chapter with this single significant example of any number of critical, class, and sexual biases that have led to the widespread, unquestioned dismissal of TV movies as so much pap. Men smirk at them, as they do at romance novels and soaps, because they deal emotionally and sometimes melodramatically with the kinds of things women have traditionally concerned themselves with—illness, family tragedy, small-scale injustice. Highbrow critics and would-be *auteurs* sneer at them because, unlike kitschy attempts like "Hill Street" to impose high-art techniques on pop genres, they adapt to the conventions they have inherited and focus more on feeling and theme than on form. TV artists themselves, when they reach a certain level of success, usually abhor them because they are so obviously and unapologetically "television" rather than theater or cinema. And network executives themselves reject their movies, even at their most serious and successful, because they have so little esteem for their own work and for their audiences.

All of these prejudices have led to the neglect of an important form. Let us look at what everyone has been missing.

2

Genre, Narrative,
and the Public Sphere

*To me, the legacy of the last eight years is very powerful. It's left
people with a desire for they don't kow what. But they know
they have this desire. Desire is the consciousness of a certain
kind of emptiness.*

Laurie Anderson, 1989

Laurie Anderson is obviously talking about the Reagan years. She
is also obviously right. But her perspective is historically limited.
In fact, this "desire for [we] don't know what" has always been
a fact of life in these United States. There has always been a promise of utopia and a failure to deliver the goods. Our collective
myths and dreams—now most prominently evident in pop culture—reflect that desire and provide moments of what feels almost like their fulfillment, "utopian moments" (Radway 1984,
215) of hope that grow out of the dimension of every form of
mass culture that, according to Fredric Jameson, "remains implicitly, and no matter how faintly, negative and critical of the social order from which, as a product and commodity, it springs"
(Jameson 1979, 144).

TV movies, even at their least interesting and most hokey, are
no exception to this essentially political truth. They are, at worst,
social fairy tales; at best, they are shattering moments of radical
insight shared by a national community. In this chapter, I want to
define the genre in terms of its aesthetic features as well as its place
in the larger historic, political, and social realm that constitutes
our public sphere.

We all know, more or less, how these dramas work. Like all

32

popular genres, they are governed by a few simple rules that grow out of their social and economic context and role. What Barry Grant has written about theatrical genres can as easily apply to telefeatures: "genre movies are those commercial feature films which, through repetition and variation, tell familiar stories with familiar characters in familiar situations" (Grant 1986, xii). So can what Thomas Schatz has written on the same theme. Acknowledging the popular genre's commercial function, its need to adhere to certain lowest-common-denominator demands, he also recognizes that genre film "represents a distinct manifestation of contemporary society's basic mythic impulse, its desire to confront elemental conflicts inherent in culture while at the same time participating in the projection of an idealized collective self-image" (Schatz 1981, 99).

But television is different from film in a lot of important ways. Its placement in the private home, where it speaks directly to a presumed family audience, its symbiotic economic and structural relationship to commercial advertising, and its immediacy— dealing with hot issues and breaking news in a dramatic fashion— dictates its particular generic rules. The myths of TV movies, the "idealized collective self-image" they project, are different from theatrical films. So are their aesthetics. In this chapter, I want to look at the standard structure of the form, at a few movies that transcend the norms, and, finally, at the way in which theatrical and TV movies differ in their treatment of similar themes. At bottom, I want to place the form in the context of a national discourse on important social issues in an age when public discourse takes place primarily—for better or for worse—on commercial television.

Although it is common to think of TV movies as falling into a very few categories—disease of the week, disaster of the week, social issue of the week, whitewashed history of the week—there are actually a lot more standard themes than that, too many to summarize here. I have chosen, therefore, to look quickly at two subgenres that are both common enough and classically simple enough to serve as maps of the territory.

Structurally, all feature-length (as opposed to miniseries, which I will address next) TV movies follow a few given rules. They all begin—and end—with the family; all other matters are subsumed into that never-questioned ideal institution. They begin with a problem or crisis that threatens, or at least has an impact on, the functioning of a nuclear family or the values that generally accrue to that idealized structure. Midpoint, the crisis escalates, but by the end of the movie it is, one way or another, resolved and family values are reinstated as inalienable and transcendent. This is true even in movies that end tragically, or in which the family does not survive intact. *The Karen Carpenter Story*, for example, ends with the death of the young celebrity heroine from causes related to her anorexia. Nonetheless, the final scenes show her "cured" and reunited with her parents (who, throughout, have been presented—albeit vaguely and superficially—as contributing to their daugher's fatal illness). Her death is attributed to past self-abuse, and the pathos is heightened by this romantic contrivance. Similarly, *The High Cost of Passion*, a docudrama about the murder of a young prostitute by a biology professor who became obsessed with her, ends with a grisly murder and then ends again, with a flashback to the victim's reconciliation with her parents and the wonderful boyfriend who waited for her. Teresa Carpenter, a journalist who covered the case, has commented on the way in which the TV version reduced the complicated case to a simple "tale of unblemished Virtue ravaged by unqualified Villainy" in order to ensure that the girl would not "lose sympathy in the eyes of a prime-time audience" (Carpenter 1990, 28). Bad girls can be bad on television only if in the end they see the error of their ways and return to the family fold.

Other movies in which families do in fact break up—and they are few and far between—nonetheless do not discard the Platonic ideal of family harmony as a kind of spiritual presence informing the sometimes contradictory events of the text. *The Burning Bed*, to name only one, valorizes a woman who actually incinerated her abusive husband. Still, her motives were familial. She acted as a mother. And there is a strong implication that, with her acquittal, she will move on to a better life and a better man.

Historical miniseries docudramas—*Winds of War, Roots, The Blue and the Gray*, and their like—do much the same thing. Their longer length and focus on a series of critical moments alters the classic structure I just outlined, of course. There is not just one dramatic conflict; there are, instead, a series of critical points. The narrative structure is thus more episodic than Aristotelian. The moments of dramatic crisis are both public and private: the hero or heroine moves back and forth between issues of history and home life. Still, while marriage and family are not their primary themes, they nonetheless manage to integrate the domestic lives of the heroes, the men who make history, with their political and historical acts. *Winds of War*, especially, reaches excesses of absurdity in its portrayal of the fictional general/hero as at once privy to every great battle and meeting of World War II and constantly rushing home to deal with the problems of his wife and children. All this is portrayed as though the two realms were linked. In fact, of course, they are. The personal is political and all that. But these movies do not understand this idea in the same way feminists do. Rather, they trivialize issues of power and money. They obliterate or mystify their representation of social, economic, and political institutions, making it seem as though individuals, acting as "family members" and according to the dictates of personal family values, actually are the agents of social and political phenomena.

Not having gotten the news that the subject is dead, that the "master narrative" of bourgeois culture no longer works, TV movies proceed in terms of nineteenth-century bourgeois realism. The big difference, of course, is that where Tolstoy and Dickens did in fact sketch out the interrelationships between the private and public spheres, TV movies, not really as innocent as they seem, can rarely afford to give even a glimpse of public reality. The postmodern moment, that point during the Nixon years when, as novelist Louis V. B. Jones nicely puts it, "things stopped meaning anything, or when things first started to mean their opposite" (Jones 1989, C21), has created a dilemma for television, or at least for its owners and sponsors. As a result, TV movies, the most public, political, and socially important of dramatic forms, have, for reasons already outlined, tended to ignore the whole explosive arena of American politics in favor of a displacement—a fantasy really—of all significant action to the private realm. Like soap operas, they disingenuously attribute all political behavior to the heroes' primary concern with private life and domestic values. They domesticate matters that are far more complex and messy than that. To the extent that they become the primary forms through which history and politics are perceived and understood by most Americans, they are a matter of serious concern. And yet, even here, there is a utopian moment to be found. Like the Beach Boys, those great California dreamers, they traffic in a metareality whose driving emotional and political force is summed up in the wistful phrase "Wouldn't it be nice . . . ?"

Many other aspects of the TV movie typify and define the genre; some of them have already been discussed. The small screen and poor quality of the image—technical matters—dictate the need for tight interior shots, lots of close-ups, and intense one-on-one exchanges. Factors that make simple stories necessary include the domestic setting in which viewing occurs, forcing any drama to compete for the attention of viewers with all the other activities that go on in a home while the television plays; the truly mass audience that is made up of all sectors of the population, even those least literate or culturally sophisticated; and the constant commercial interruptions that not only break the narrative flow but also encourage zapping to other channels. Every scene must further the action, every piece of dialogue must give clear information about plot, theme, and character. Finally, the settings themselves, the mise-en-scène, which serves, on the simplest level, as a set of signs indicating the values and meanings of the action, must be coloring-book clear both visually and symbolically. For one thing, there is the matter of picture quality. For another, there is the commercial angle. *Things* are important in TV narrative because they are what sponsors are selling and because there is no time to deal in symbolism of a complex kind. Audiences "know" what certain items mean because we have all learned the codes. To deal in ambiguity or nuance is to risk losing ratings.

This may sound awful, but I am playing devil's advocate here. The real significance of this "low art" form is its very accessibility, its way of allowing an entire nation—at least 25 percent of which is functionally illiterate—to participate in a common cultural and political experience. All TV movies are not, of course, interesting or even worth viewing for any reason. Many are simply awful and many are politically dangerous. Even the best of them have reactionary elements, if you want to be pure about it. Nonetheless, they are crucially important to understand because, unlike sitcoms and other series television, they deal with serious issues of the moment. I am going to start, then, by analyzing two of the most pedestrian, but also most classic, examples in order to illustrate how the form works at its least compelling.

The ABCs of the Telefeature

My Mother's Secret Life is a fictional account of a call girl's transformation to wholesome wife and mother. *Robert F. Kennedy and His Times* is a standard Great Man biography. In both, the qualities that have made TV movies grist for the mills of those who believe television to be a wasteland are more than apparent. And yet, even here, there are reasons for audience fascination and involvement, in spite of the sexual and political bad faith of the movies.

In *My Mother's Secret Life*, a prosperous call girl's life is disrupted when the daughter she left with her ex-husband suddenly appears on her doorstep after the untimely death of her father. At first the woman is simply stunned. She pretends to be a businesswoman of some kind and plans to get rid of the young teenager as soon as she can figure out how. Gradually, the girl wins her affection. At midpoint in the movie, of course, the daughter figures things out and, also predictably, in a moment of despair and self-contempt decides to follow in her mother's footsteps. Mom's eyes are opened, her maternal instincts are awakened, and she resolves to change her life. Out go the furs and silk teddies; on go the jeans and work shirts. As luck—or television—would have it, one of her johns, a nice rich guy seriously in love with her, marries her and they become a family.

This is standard genre stuff with little nuance of any kind. The plot progresses all too obviously from the disruption of both principals' lives to imminent catastrophe to a happily-ever-after ending. As in all TV movies, there are no scenes that do not further the plot. The settings, too, are standard and typical: first the poor but happy life on the farm with Dad, then the swank glamour of high-rise heaven, and finally the suburban house with picket fence. The mise-en-scène is always emblematic and obvious. Close-ups and tight interiors make the reading of the text unambiguous and transparent. People act and change on the basis of intense moments of insight and emotion. We never get below the surface. The ending is improbable, to say the least.

So what is the appeal? This fluff piece is actually moving. It is, without question, pure melodrama. It reeks of sentimentality. But, as Lynn Joyrich has pointed out, "melodrama's popularity has historically coincided with times of intense social and ideological crisis" (Joyrich 1987, 135). She lists among the many contradictions that characterize our current crisis and that are typically the stuff of melodrama those between "topicality and timelessness, public and private, the Law and desire" and she notes, quite rightly, that "TV melodrama is ideally suited to reveal the subtle strains of bourgeois culture" and its many contradictions.

It is these contradictions—particularly that between "the Law and desire"—that this pedestrian movie addresses and, in its thoroughly hokey way, seems to resolve. But its power can be appreciated only if we view it in terms of social context, of its place as an event in the public sphere, where issues of desire and repression, of the contradiction between sexuality and motherhood, are addressed. Since TV movies always focus on the family as the "natural" condition of life, the happy ending is a given. Still, there is something incredibly attractive about Loni Anderson, who plays the mother, as we see her in her own milieu. While the dominant text plays her as cold, mercenary, "unnatural" in her isolation, her refusal to connect with her ex-husband and child, a subtext contradicts that message. She is also independent, self-confident, and lacking in sexual hypocrisy. She knows who she is and seems pretty much content with the hard choices she has made. She is also, of course, glamorous and rich. To her gawky daughter, she is the essence of poise and polish.

The form of the movie, personal and intimate, insists that we go through it in her stiletto-heeled shoes. This is a fantasy of radical sexual freedom and its (sometime) rewards that is easy to take. If there is a utopian moment in this film, it is the moment when the daughter accepts her mother's life and still loves her, as a mother. This is a reconciliation of a contradiction that, in fact, is not reconcilable in a sexist society.

The necessary conclusion notwithstanding, what this movie

does is to personalize, sentimentally of course, a social issue that is generally treated sensationally or with moral opprobrium. What it leaves out, what it fudges, what it simply lies about—all this makes it a far from ideal treatment of its subject. But in following rigidly the conventions of its genre, it brings to the domestic sphere a representation of sex work that is humanized and understandable. Like the daytime talk shows that feature sexually titillating topics and allow the audiences—in the studio and at home—to get involved in issues that are normally taboo in "polite company," this movie demystifies its topic. It merges the good girl/bad girl split in a way that is—I am certain—reassuring to many women for whom this split has caused anxiety and concern.

Robert F. Kennedy and His Times is a very different commodity. It treats real political and historical events in terms of personal and family life and in so doing obscures and mystifies matters of serious public concern. If *My Mother's Secret Life* cleans up and almost valorizes prostitution, leaving out the pimps, the degradation, the exploitation that are the realities of most streetwalkers' lives, it does give women a glimpse of a fantasy world of sexual and economic freedom. The public role of movies like *RFK* is a bit more problematic. Still, it too fulfills a utopian fantasy of what public life could be if the contradictions between the public and private spheres, between wealth and power on the one hand and poverty and powerlessness on the other, were resolved.

As is typical of these Great Man epics, *RFK* takes liberties with history and with its hero's private life. Unlike the two-hour telefeature, the historical miniseries, while always focusing on public figures as, first and foremost, family members, is episodic in its narrative structure. The hero is seen as a child, an adolescent, and finally a public figure tackling a series of political hurdles that are handled with grace and are always overcome. Kennedy associate John Siegenthaler has said that the drama's portrayal of Bobby is accurate. "His love of family, his unswerving loyalty, and his passion for social justice come across accurately," he insists (Siegenthaler 1985, 1D), although actual events and situations are often invented, deleted, and distorted. To be sure. The Bay of Pigs affair, a botched attack on Cuba, which Bobby helped his brother John plan, to use one glaring example, is simply not mentioned. What is shown is a series of encounters and dilemmas Kennedy faced nobly and victoriously. A persona is created, one that stands for all things liberal and progressive, especially in 1985—the height of the Reagan years—when the drama was aired. Kennedy is seen fighting for black civil rights, for economic and political, rather than military, policies in Southeast Asia and Latin America, and other good things.

If there is a flaw in this martyred saint's character, it is that he lacks the glibness and charisma of his older brother. This allows the audience to see him as someone "just like us." In fact—and here is where the family angle comes in—the structure of the movie is a series of scenes cutting up and back between the public world of national and international affairs and the "Leave It to Beaver" world of home. Every political issue and problem is talked over with the ever maternal, ever supportive Ethel. Bobby is endlessly cuddling babies, changing diapers, giving bottles. His public life is quite clearly an extension of his private life; they are a seamless whole and he is the most whole and wholesome of men.

Even before the publicity about Bobby's affair with Marilyn Monroe, this picture is too good to be true. It is downright cloying, but it appeals to a national fantasy of how things ought to be in a functioning democracy. Most obviously, it heals the contradiction between public and private life. It downplays the role of wealth and power in the Kennedy dynasty in favor of a just-folks view of the ruling class and our political leaders. Coming as it did in the Reagan years, it is a disingenuous but clear statement of liberal values. Ideologically, it is of course rather contemptible in its many lies and its three cheers for the Great Man—the Great Rich Man—theory of history. But at this point I am not reading ideologically in that sense. I am describing the way in which TV movies intervene in the public sphere, become part of national ideology and debate, and manage, even at their soppiest, to engage us. Moreover, I am mapping out a dialectic of the genre in which, even at its worst, there is a war between reactionary and progressive tendencies that is neatly resolved through narrative strategy. The parameters of that dialectic are clearly drawn and limited to certain, at best, liberal values because the public sphere itself is never mapped. Rather, it is implicitly denied in favor of a personal, individualistic sense of how even progressive change occurs.

TV movies simply do not portray a political or economic world in any meaningful sense. The issue of prostitution, for example, is not presented in terms of economic necessity or even of sexism. It is presented in strictly psychological and emotional terms. The Loni Anderson character has shut down emotionally; that is why she can function as a call girl. If she let her emotions out—as she eventually does—the implication is clear: she would not do this cold-blooded, mercenary kind of work. The fact is that most prostitutes actually are single mothers who can't get child care during the day and turn to "the life" because it alone among unskilled women's job options allows them to be mothers to their children. And that is just the women who work in brothels and massage parlors. Streetwalkers are predominantly drug addicts whose needs drive them to this work for obvious reasons. TV movies, however, favor classy call girls in need of shrinks or husbands, or teenage runaways whose dysfunctional families force them out into the cold world against their wills. They invariably end up with a new or revamped happy family. All's well that ends well.

In the Kennedy series, the obfuscation of the public sphere and of economic and political realities is more obvious and more insidious. Like the rest of the media, and mainstream culture generally, it pretends that politicians operate as individualistic heroes and get their primary identity from their family role. Money, corporations, even government institutions are virtually ignored. The Kennedy involvement in the Bay of Pigs incident is only the most glaring example of the way in which public realities are denied in the interest of personal domestic drama. We never see how any institution works in these series, nor do we ever— heaven forbid—see the dark side of the Kennedy game, the deals, duplicities, and compromises that every successful Washington politician participates in. Most glaringly, we do not see anything even vaguely resembling collective action. The civil rights movement, the antiwar movement, these do not exist in TV land. It is always *Bad Day at Black Rock* there, a larger-than-life hero taking on the bad guys one on one and restoring peace and justice.

To the extent that these dramas do enter the public sphere, they are nonetheless political statements that become important players in the realm of social discourse on the subjects they treat.

They matter because they affect consciousness, personal debate, and public debate. To the extent that we have some form of democratic society, they represent an important element in the process by which personal opinion, social debate, and political decisions are made or formed. Since our democratic structures are tainted, to say the least, and the media, in particular, do a lot of what the Frankfurt School always said they did—create false consciousness and manipulate audiences by obscuring the very economic and political interests they serve—there is a need for left critiques.

On the other hand, media analysis has come a long way since the days of cultural theorist Theodor Adorno. Leftist writers like Antonio Gramsci and Raymond Williams and the cultural studies schools they have inspired have told us much about the contradictions of the media, their way of preserving hegemony by incorporating, tolerating, recuperating—the favored term depends upon one's particular willingness to give the devil his due—alternative visions and readings. Reader response theory has also contributed to our growing sophistication about how texts are received and used, how contradictions within any given text can lead to at least partially progressive readings. While some of this theory has in my view gone way too far (see Radway 1984 and Marc 1984), giving readers much more power to create their own text than is in fact realistic, it has nonetheless offered a powerful tool for seeing media products as arenas for ideological struggle rather than merely as top-down manipulation.

Most significantly, when one looks at the actual workings of TV production, as we did in the preceding chapter, one sees the possibility of real struggle within the networks themselves. There are more progressive people—left-liberals to be specific—working in the media than leftists and academics realize. The money is more than good, of course, a factor that works against political idealism, to be sure. But there is something else about working in television—or any other popular form—that makes a lot of political sense: you reach a mass audience. Here is where the public sphere issue comes in. To work in television, compromises and sellouts notwithstanding, is to participate in a powerful national discourse that few "high art" forms offer.

The value of neither alternative nor "high" art is in question here. Artists do in fact make choices about audience and technique all the time, and each choice has rewards and limits. I am concerned merely with establishing a rationale for a set of choices not generally understood as valuable or even legitimate. One rationale for working in television, particularly in the "long form," as the TV movie is called, is just this legitimate desire to enter the public sphere in a significant way, to have one's vision—mediated as it must be by the language and form through which television communicates its kind of master narrative—experienced and discussed by many millions of people as well as in the major forms of media itself, the local and national TV news, local and national newspapers, *TV Guide, Time,* and *Newsweek.* Through this process art does in fact become part of public discourse in a meaningful, because it is on a large scale, sense.

I chose the two movies I analyzed here because they are not only typical but also, by any conventional dramatic or political standards, among the worst of the genre. Feminists and leftists alike must cringe at the valorization of traditional marriage and of the Kennedys in dramas that treat such serious matters as sex work and U.S. government policies. Still, because media products do reflect fascinating ideological contradictions and because, given the generic framework within which they must operate, a surprising number of telefeatures manage to push the limits of the form in progressive directions, there is a lot more good news than most people realize. Nor is the good news merely ideological in the abstract theoretical sense. One of the greatest strengths of TV movies, even the worst of them, is their unvarnished schmaltziness. By sticking to personal narratives, by shamelessly (in the eyes of certain critics) playing to raw emotion and audience identification with the characters, they often make a case for their "messages" that is so moving it is hard to forget. Many have an intensity and passion that makes their intervention in the public sphere potentially explosive. I want to talk about three of them now.

Sometimes They Almost Get It Right

My sense of the intellectual and emotional impact of TV movies is impressionistic, based largely on personal conversations and shared viewing with friends and family. When I use *The Women's Room* in classes, the students (mostly female, since the course I teach is a women's studies course in representations of women in media) are enthralled. They actually do not want to leave class and wait two days for the conclusion. This I attribute to two of the film's qualities. First, it engages viewers in the lives of the characters; it makes them care. Second, it provides facts about women's history, about what it was like to come of age in the fifties, when the experience of sex, marriage, and childbirth were mostly degrading.

Beyond that, it presents a collective, if compressed, view of its subject. Set against the background of fifties suburbia and then sixties political upheaval, it follows a group of typical, maybe stereotypical, women facing the world together. It touches on mental illness, economic equality, lesbianism, and many other subjects. My students, liberated eighties achievers all, had never experienced that kind of world. Most amazing to me is always the way in which these young women respond to the ending of the film. Mira, the heroine, having survived a bad divorce, the loss of her sons, and the trauma of returning to graduate school in middle age, finds a "perfect man" at last. He is young, bright, sexy, and a "hunk." He loves her passionately and introduces her to sexual pleasure. Yet when he receives a grant to go to Africa she refuses to follow him and give up her own work. In the last scene she is lecturing to a class much like the one I teach. She gives an impassioned, upbeat lecture on the joys of women's liberation, with or without a man, and receives a standing ovation.

I always expect my students to question her choice. After all, they are part of the generation that believes in having it all and thinks of marriage and children in much more traditional ways than we did back then. But no, they are with Mira all the way. She always wanted a career and that, they insist, is quite rightly her first priority.

I relate this long anecdote because it speaks to the power of this genre to educate and to move viewers against the grain of what seems to be the dominant value system even in these most reactionary of times. The three movies I want to analyze here all have that same power. They get it partly through their use of generic conventions with which everyone is familiar. But there is a second quality they share with *The Women's Room*. They manage—unlike the Kennedy and prostitution movies—to use these conventions in a context that is far more politicized, more aware of and overtly critical of, the larger historic and political world in which they are set.

Two contextual matters need to be addressed before we look at these dramas. First, I am not arguing that these movies are free of the reactionary elements that characterize all TV drama. They are not revolutionary tracts by a long shot. At best, like the best of all television, they are a bit to the left of corporate liberalism. Their power and importance comes from something else, from their ability to enter the public sphere and arouse deep passion about political injustice. That is all they can do on their own. Texts do not organize, demonstrate, take up arms. They are merely one increasingly important player in the world of public discourse and debate that in some indirect way affects public actions. And even on that level, they are filled with the contradictions and less than radical elements that go with the commercial TV territory. They always show what the media likes to refer to as "both sides" of every issue, and even at their most political they fall far short of radical critiques.

On a more theoretical level, there is the question of when and where one sees these films. As the proponents of hermeneutics have taught us, every text is historically specific and means different things at different times. With television this problem is particularly vivid because telefeatures, unless they are so successful that they are rerun or distributed to video rental stores, are rarely seen after their initial airings. In order to analyze them properly, then, one must view them as existing on two parallel planes. As national discourses on current issues, they have one kind of meaning and effect. Viewed retrospectively, as I continuously view them as a teacher and writer, they mean something quite different. Many of the movies I discuss in this book, because they are so powerful, have entered the realm of classic texts, widely viewed and reviewed. Others are too recent to have reached that level and still others are too pedestrian to be remembered, much less reviewed and discussed in historic terms. I will keep this distinction in mind throughout my analyses and address it as a factor in audience response to the films and their impact on public life.

45

Proceeding chronologically, I will begin with *Kent State*, which was aired in early 1981, and then I will discuss the 1989 movie *Roe v. Wade*, which was shown on the eve of the historic Supreme Court decision on abortion in *Missouri v. Webster* in July of that year. These dramas are unique both in their emotional, dramatic power and in their blatant critiques of the workings of state, social, and cultural institutions, including, in one case, the male left.

I had seen *Kent State*—the docudrama about the gunning down by National Guard troops of four young people on an Ohio campus during the heated days following the 1971 invasion of Cambodia—when it originally ran on television. At the time, I found it surprisingly sympathetic to student radicals but hardly a radical film. It was, after all, only the beginning of the Reagan years and the full impact of what would happen to social life and public discourse in the next decade was far from obvious.

Now that it is available in video rental stores, I have viewed it several times recently and found myself amazed at its power and significance. It holds up well, for reasons of style, structure, and a rather sophisticated narrative strategy, as an object lesson in what "the sixties"—at their romantic, rather than political, best— really meant in ways I could never have guessed would even be necessary a mere decade later. Vietnam movies come and go these days, of course. But even the best of them focus on the very ambiguous issue of the experiences of veterans, not on the role of our government in the war—over there or here at home. *Kent State* does. For that reason its place in the discussion of television and the public sphere is more complicated than that of the more recent films I will discuss. Its importance is not, at this point, in its role as prime-time "media event" intervening in public discourse on a current event. That is not because Vietnam is old news, however. On the contrary, it is as much a matter of urgent concern today as it ever was, but for different reasons. We have a generation of kids who, as they say, don't have a clue about this whole period and are starving for information. If we who were there feel nostalgia for those days, our children and our students, coming of age in the time of the yuppie, feel an intense kind of envy for what they sense—mostly through their love of sixties music, which has never died out and is now as popular as ever among a lot of kids—was a better time to be young. *Kent State* confirms that vague sense in its portrayal of student life as well as the urgency it projects about the political situation of the time and the immediacy of involvement that was—with all its political failings and flaws—quite real for many.

The difference between viewing *Kent State* now and viewing current movies of the week is that it must be viewed—like all old movies—in TV reruns that are not given the promotion and hype of new movies, or privately, on the VCR. I make this distinction because it is important in terms of viewer experience. Like *The Women's Room*, this movie explodes into early nineties consciousness as a startling piece of recovered history, seen through the eyes of the participants. Because of its political stance, it would never be made today. It is dated, and yet it is also rather thrilling.

What puts this movie several rungs above the standard telefeature is, first of all, its focus on mass activity, both by the students and by the agencies of power. To be sure, it focuses, as is necessary, on the personalities of the four victims. None of them is "political." One is a flower child whose life centers mainly on her relationship with her live-in boyfriend. One is an ROTC student for whom the military is the only way he can afford a college education. One is a nice girl interested in child development, and the last is a social misfit with no clear take on any of the political issues.

We become emotionally involved with these kids. We like them all and feel horror at their senseless deaths. None, even the one in ROTC, is in favor of the war, and as things heat up even he is tormented by the behavior of the government and the military he is committed to serving. The device of involving us, emotionally, with these apolitical kids—a device that struck me, in 1981, as a cop-out—now seems absolutely right. That is because, from a historical and personal distance, it is the transformation of these straight kids, and their martyrdom, that most poignantly illustrates what happened to that generation—why so many became so wildly radical, took up behavior that placed them squarely in the middle of an actual public sphere, a world of political action by individual citizens that affected, quite explosively, national and global events.

If the movie stuck only to these kids, however, it would not work politically at all. What the producers did, instead, was to give an enormous amount of footage to the ominously inevitable clash of two political forces—the student organizers and their followers, and the state and its military arm. Structurally, in true docudrama form, the movie traces the escalation of brute force, but not by showing one "bad guy" but a whole set of them. In this way it manages to portray a real public sphere in which people act not as isolated moral agents but as members of a broad group. The governor of Ohio appears as a veritable madman, intent on breaking the student revolt by any means necessary. But he is not alone. The university chancellor supports him; many of the faculty, by passive default, do too. And then there is the National Guard, an odd mix of brutal young bigots eager for students' blood and nice kids who gradually realize what they have gotten themselves into and in some cases actually break down and bolt. There are also, of course, the older, tougher pros who really hate the kids and whose blood lust is as vicious as it is realistic. Anyone who lived through those times will feel a shock of recognition as the mixed but essentially innocent students move closer and closer to a murderous confrontation with an authority whose confidence is so shaky that it is both irrational and reckless. I stress this aspect of the movie because it is sometimes difficult to remember that such things actually happened to nice white middle-class kids, and it is surely impossible for the nice white middle-class kids of today to imagine such a possibility. In that sense, the movie is something of a horror film, and it has the same impact; it incites shock, fear, and amazement at the possibility of something almost supernaturally evil really happening. The difference, of course, is that this is no fantasy. Its realism, its historic documentation, and the coda that explains that no one was ever prosecuted or punished for these murders are all too compelling, and so are the intimacy and involvement that the televisual apparatus creates, for reasons of technical and aesthetic necessity (see Ellis 1982, Part II, for a thorough analysis of the workings of broadcast television in terms of televisual apparatus).

Dramatically, the verbal confrontations between these two

forces are true to life. So are the reactions of the student radicals. At one point, for example, the young white woman who is the primary organizer of the demonstrations becomes ill when she realizes that the guard is firing real ammunition at the unarmed kids. In a state of shock she mumbles "The guns were really loaded" to a black student activist. "The guns are always loaded," he replies with some contempt for her innocence.

At another point, a student who continues to bait the guard, in the same kind of innocence, says to the most Ramboesque of them, "I can't understand you. I don't hate you, I pity you. Not for what you are but for what you'll never be." This speech invokes an aching sense of what was very real and most endearing about the student movement and is almost unfathomable today: naively, it believed in a utopian vision. This is not simply a "utopian moment." It is a summing up of something that actually existed for a lot of people for a lot of years: a belief in utopian possibility and a radical refusal to conform to what was then quite obviously a corrupt and brutal state.

Corruption in high places is a given today, of course, but utopian opposition is not, certainly not in the media. From "Dynasty" and "Dallas" to "Miami Vice" and *Scarface*, cynicism and even nihilism reign supreme as even the "liberal" response to institutional corruption. Watching the Iran-contra hearings was nothing like watching the Watergate hearings. The sense that neither the media nor the government was anything more than an Orwellian phantom colored even the juiciest testimony of Ollie North and friends. No one really expected anything real or good to come of these hearings. They were, at best, entertainment, good for some laughs. Watergate was a different matter entirely. Coming as a result of the very different political world of the sixties and early seventies—the world *Kent State* maps in part—it could be viewed as a triumph for our side. Nixon actually had to resign, after all; Reagan and Bush were never in such danger. Who would have orchestrated a movement for impeachment? Who would have believed in it enough to join?

I do not want to overstress the significance of this movie, however. It is still not a truly radical critique, nor is it ultimately even utopian in its dominant political projection. For one thing, it is not about radical democracy, even at its most utopian. It is about idealism; about good guys and bad guys. It still has a conciliatory white liberal professional—a professor—who speaks for the film's point of view, the most radical element of which is the idea that the university should have issued a statement opposing the war. Most importantly, it does not end with utopia, or even victory for the students. It ends horribly and thus, structurally, undercuts its own element of political and imaginative utopianism. According to Northrop Frye's generic catgories, it is not a comedy but a tragedy. The horror of seeing the dead bodies of kids randomly gunned down on a college campus and then learning that no one was punished is enough to defuse any hope for an actual revival of mass radical action. It does exist in history and society however, and for that reason, like the many other movies that to a lesser degree confront public issues seriously, it stands as a powerful emotional and political experience, one that at least makes real the possibility of an imaginary that is radically utopian.

Andreas Huyssen has written eloquently about the power of "Hollywood type fictionalization" to affect audiences in profound political ways and has suggested that left and avant-garde critics might learn something from the conventions of this much-maligned work. Speaking about the enormous success of the American miniseries *Holocaust* in West Germany, he credits the use of personal family drama as a way of confronting the horrors of the time with the series success. "*Holocaust* was not only a major media event," he writes, "but, more importantly, a social psychological event." The "narrative strategy" of forcing German viewers to see the holocaust through the eyes of a single Jewish family, he believes, "places us on the side of the victim, makes us suffer with them and fear the killers" (Huyssen 1986, 98). This is exactly what *Kent State* does, and its effect is equally startling and unnerving. This strategy also characterizes *Roe v. Wade*, although the timing of its presentation creates a very different viewing experience.

In discussing *Roe v. Wade* we move more squarely into the workings of the movie of the week and its way of creating a mediated public sphere that intervenes in actual public discourse. This docudrama about the historic Supreme Court ruling that legalized abortion in 1972 ran in May of 1989, about a month before the Supreme Court was again scheduled to make an important decision about abortion rights, one that, in the long run, could set a precedent by which everything feminists fought for nearly twenty years ago could be taken from us.

For the first time in several years, feminists began once more to organize and demonstrate in an effort to mobilize public opinion and educate young people about the seriousness of the threat posed to women's rights by the Reagan/Bush administrations. Unlike *Kent State*, then, *Roe* appeared on the scene—on the screen—in the midst of a very real political crisis whose outcome was far from clear. Its role as an actor in this crisis was quite real.

In order to understand just how this movie fit into the larger public discourse, we need to look at certain facts about the way it was made and presented. In fact, the televisual apparatus that defines and molds this form is very important in understanding *Roe*'s dramatic and social effect. It is a wonderful case history of how television works, how its intriguing contradictions get worked out, and, most clearly, how institution, form, and content are inseparable in the reading of TV texts.

First of all, it was a judgment call, and something of a risky one at that, for NBC to decide to run this movie at this time. On the one hand, abortion was certainly a hot issue. On the other hand, though, this particular treatment of the topic was definitely biased in favor of the two female protagonists, Ellen Russell (a pseudonym for Norma McCorvey, the woman who acted as "Jane Roe" in the case that finally made abortion legal) and her lawyer, Sara Weddington.

The network was well aware of the difficulties and of the high costs of offending viewers and especially sponsors. In fact, like other controversial movies—most dramatically *The Women's Room* and *The Day After*—this one ran at a loss to the network because of last-minute sponsor bolts. What the network lost in immediate revenues it hoped to recover in future earnings, however, since the movie ran during sweeps month—the month in which advertising rates are determined on the basis of ratings—and high ratings would guarantee higher advertising revenues for future programming. Nonetheless, at a time when right-wing lobbyists were getting lots of publicity and sponsor reaction in their crusades against "offensive" programs—particularly those that defiled the sanctity of traditional marriage and family values—*Roe* must certainly have contributed to a lot of ulcers in NBC's executive offices. Perhaps most interesting is the fact that this project had been in the works for five years but had never before been scheduled to run. Again, the judgments of the network heads reflected a sense that the issue would draw audiences at this particular moment. They were counting, to some extent, on the star status of the two principals, Amy Madigan as Sara and Holly Hunter as Ellen. In the years since the project was first discussed, both had become big-time movie stars, no longer dependent on TV movies but still willing to do this one because—as is often the case with telefeatures—the female roles were juicier and more serious than those in most theatrical scripts.

Potentially sabotaging this very strength, however, the actual writing of the script gradually worked to downplay the very charisma of its stars. It went through seventeen rewrites—an inordinate number even for Hollywood. Each one, according to Alison Cross, who wrote them, gave more and more time and sympathy to the state's "prolife" positions and proponents, while "toning down" the Weddington character to make her less charismatic and attractive. Moreover, as we shall see when we look at the text itself, the movie's ideological contortions are quite clever. Far from coming off as against motherhood or for sexual freedom as a value in and of itself, the movie states its case for abortion rights in terms of Ellen's maternal feelings, her agony at having to give up a child for adoption and live, forever after, with the knowledge that she has a child somewhere she will never know. That is a valid position, of course, but it is also more compatible with right-wing ideology than is usual in arguments for abortion rights. It plays to the obsession with children that characterized the eighties, when missing children's pictures appeared on milk cartons and the media concern with child abuse reached near-epidemic proportions.

What ultimately made this movie's impact so strongly prochoice was its dramatic strategies. For one thing, the two excellent actresses in the lead roles biased the drama. It is the nature of dramatic presentation to put the viewer in the protagonists' shoes—a simple matter of point of view. It is through Ellen's, and to a lesser extent Sara's, eyes that we experience this drama and they, especially Ellen, are irresistibly likable and sincere.

Ellen is seen first as a carnival barker living hand to mouth from one menial job to the next. She has already given one child to her mother to raise, after her husband ran out on her. She is feisty, rebellious, a bit of a hard liver, and she is virtually denied access to her daughter because her mother dislikes and disapproves of her. Let me emphasize again that these are not the qualities that make for theatrical film heroines. Working-class women of "loose" sexual morals rarely get to be heroines on the big screen, at least in Hollywood. But Ellen is portrayed as very much a heroine, in traditional dramatic terms. A self-described "loner"—"I don't mess with nobody and I don't like nobody messing with me"— she agrees to be the complainant Sara and her associate are seeking because she wants a safe abortion. Midway through the movie, however, having lost the case in Texas, she delivers and gives up her baby without ever touching it or knowing its sex. From then on, her involvement in the case as it goes to the Supreme Court is strictly a matter of principle. "It's the first time in my life I ever did anything for someone else," she tells the attorneys.

Another important aspect of Ellen's character is her fantasy of "bein' somebody someday." As a child she imagined herself a movie star. As an adult she fantasizes that her abusive ex-husband will someday pick up a newspaper and read about her having done some great thing while "he's still pumping gas." This is the note on which the movie ends: a girlfriend tells Ellen that she read in the paper that "they just made abortion legal." Ellen grabs the paper and blurts out what she had never told anyone before, for fear of disapproval, that she is "Jane Roe." Her friend, dumbfounded, stares at her in awe. "Girl, you really done something," she says. "How 'bout a beer?" Then we fade to a final freeze-frame of Ellen smiling with pride. That, in Northrop Frye's terms, definitely qualifies as a comic ending.

In counterpoint to Ellen's story is the very different narrative of Sara's battle with the legal system and the male left. Here the movie pushes the boundaries of the genre to bring in at least some sense of a women's movement as a major force in mobilizing for this case. Sara has never argued a case before when she finds herself on the way to the Supreme Court. As she prepares, we hear— in typical TV movie didactic style—the primary arguments for the right to abortion. Staying close to historic accuracy, the movie places Sara in the middle of a political situation that is hard to remember in these days of at least lip service to women's rights by everyone in the public arena, a time when men did not take feminism seriously, to say the least.

Again, this film recreates a history that is lost to most young people and forgotten by many older ones. Ellen's attempts to get an illegal abortion and her horror at the filthy, badly equipped "clinic" she goes to and then runs from are at least a mild picture of what it was like for women a mere twenty years ago. (That it is only a mild picture is a function of the bizarre workings of the networks. Shots of blood on the floor and mentions of coat hangers were ruled unacceptable by NBC's standards and practices people. The irony of this, when one considers the bloodshed and abuse of women that are standard prime-time fare, is macabre.)

Meanwhile, back in the professional legal community, Sara experiences a different kind of sexism when she turns for help to a group that obviously represents the New York Center for Constitutional Rights. Promising to help write the brief with her, the male honchos of the left pretty much abandon her in favor of cases dealing with civil rights and antiwar protests. What is significant here is the resonance of truth that these scenes—like those in *Kent State*—carry. Any woman who lived through the fifties and sixties knows exactly what at least one, if not both, of these experiences were like. Whether getting an illegal abortion or trying to convince male activists that women's issues mattered, women experienced a kind of suffering and humiliation that—whatever the state of women now—simply does not happen in quite that way today.

The power of this narrative is in its integration of ideology and raw emotion, its ability to explain matters of history and theory while arousing absolute rage in a lot of viewers, especially female viewers. This emotional response is what makes these movies matter. My own casual test of the effectiveness of individual telefeatures is always the conversations I get into the next day. The women I work with, those who are not contemptuous of television, have visceral responses to these films and a great desire to talk to me—because they know of my interest in TV movies—

about them. If I were doing the kinds of surveys done by audience response theorists I could be more scientific about these conversations. Since I am not, I have to report very limited findings based on small random samples. But it is the emotional and intellectual excitement of my colleagues—especially students and secretaries—that most interests me and convinces me of the correctness of my approach. For a day or two, at least, there is an enormous, sometimes passionate, involvement in the issues. Older women feel the outrage I feel; students express amazement that such things could have happened.

This brings me back to the larger issue of the intervention of TV movies into the public sphere. Institutionally, the networks themselves provide this context by linking dramatic presentations of social issues with discussions by "experts" that often follow the movies. But these are orchestrated by the networks and are made to fit within ideological and emotional limits that characterize "serious" TV discourse. In the case of *Roe*, there was a debate, moderated by Tom Brokaw, between two antiabortion activists and two prochoice advocates. There was a lot of anger and emotion in this debate, mostly from the right-wing spokespeople and the audience. Much of it was aimed at Brokaw, who, as NBC representative, was accused of running a proabortion program. Since the limits of these kinds of discourses are always, at the left flank, liberalism, while the right is allowed—or takes—greater ideological liberty, there were no radical feminist speakers and no feminist rage. The audience, however, as in the daytime talk shows about sexual and feminist issues, was under no such constraint and there were at least a few angry voices heard from there. In fact, it was clear that Brokaw himself was more than a little shaken by the outbursts. A network news anchor, he found himself in a situation much closer to the kind of thing that happens on less prestigious, less intellectually respectable shows like "The Oprah Winfrey Show" and "Geraldo." He clearly did not like it.

I don't want to overstate the power of this discussion. The network naturally screens participants, audience members, and questions for these events, thereby limiting and programming the nature of the discourse (see Tuchman 1978, 119-36). In daily life, people have much more interesting and emotionally vital discussions of these movies than Ted Koppel does. It is not the "experts' " views that most strongly affect the real world. The movies themselves do that, and the networks, in attempting to cool down this factor, to end on a note of rational, expert, institutionally sanctioned interpretation, quite clearly act to defuse the powerful effects of the "entertainment" aspect of their movies. But these features are not mere entertainment, of course. They are, as I have said, complex composites of three kinds of experience: emotional drama, ideological discourse, and social event.

Does Hollywood Do It Better?

Before we leave this discussion of how TV movies, generically, work, one more issue needs to be addressed: the difference between the way theatrical films and TV movies present similar themes. In order to understand the aesthetic parameters of the TV movie genre and its divergence from the classic Hollywood form that precedes it generically, we must compare the two. Such a comparison also speaks to the high art/low art controversy implicit in all discussion of television. I do not intend to compare telefeatures with the kinds of films generally thought of as "art films." I intend, rather, to discuss popular, but nonetheless important, Hollywood movies that are discussed in a critically serious way. That classic Hollywood films are, in fact, today considered worthy of intricate analyses and classroom exposition is itself interesting. After all, it was not long ago that film itself was considered too "popular" and "low brow" to be treated with anything but disdain. Those days are over now for film but not, unfortunately, for television.

How did film arrive at its currently respectable position? In the same way that television of certain kinds is now being taken increasingly seriously: because some people began looking at it with greater interest and scrutiny and finding value in it not visible to those with elitist perspectives. This is of course what I am attempting to do with the telefeature. Let us see how it compares with its more revered relative.

In making this comparison, I have chosen to analyze two films, one made for television, the other theatrical, both dealing with the same kind of issue—a middle-class family crisis involving a troubled teenager. The subject, and even the narrative structures, of these two works are far more typical of television than theatrical drama. Nonetheless, when Hollywood does deal with such issues—usually in times of social upheaval and changing lifestyle patterns—it treats the subject matter differently in subtle ways, as these two films indicate.

The theatrical film *Ordinary People* deals with a nuclear family in the midst of a crisis and centers on a single family member, in this case the mother, as the ultimate cause of the problem. *Sarah T.—Portrait of a Teenage Alcoholic* is a telefeature about a family torn apart by the alcoholism of the daughter. That the issue is, in this case, so easy to spell out is indicative of the primary difference between serious theatrical films and TV movies. *Ordinary People*, while far from complex, is not easy to sum up in a word or phrase. It is more emotionally convoluted and dense. But TV movies, with their need to be capsulized in a word or phrase for purposes of promotion as well as accessibility to audiences, cannot afford even this level of subtlety (Rapping 1987, 142–46).

Sarah T. and *Ordinary People* are actually quite similar in many ways. In fact, *Ordinary People* could conceivably have been made as a TV movie. The plot reads like one: An affluent, apparently happy suburban family suffers a tragedy. The elder son is killed in a boating accident. The younger, a high school student, survives the accident and, filled with guilt, attempts suicide. The film focuses on the aftermath of the suicide attempt and traces the young man's recovery—through therapy, a new girlfriend, and his father's growing understanding and support.

Watching this film unfold, one has the sense that it could easily have been a telefeature. TV movies about suicide, incest, and AIDS have in many ways resembled *Ordinary People*. It is middle-class domestic drama of the kind television loves. From the early establishing shots of the young man, Conrad, singing in a church choir to the careful focus on the interior of the Jarrett home, the oak and silver, the L. L. Bean look of comfort and security, we are drawn into the interior of a family whose veneer, as every detail signals, is about to be stripped away through crisis.

The narrative structure is in many ways similar to television. A family member is targeted as, if not the villain, at least the cause of the disruption of family harmony and well-being. In this case—and here we have something that is quite rare on TV—the "bad" parent is the mother, Beth, who is portrayed as cold, controlling, and shallow. She has favored the dead son and cannot forgive Conrad for having survived and then, adding insult to injury, causing a scandal by attempting suicide. As in TV movies, the father comes to a realization of what Conrad has not been given and what he needs. But it is hardly the mother who facilitates this transformation, as she would do on television. In fact, the structural detail most radically different from television is the conclusion in which Beth, the bad mother, is actually banished rather than reconstructed.

Two stylistic elements of this film in particular highlight the greatest differences between television's treatment of family matters and that of theatrical films. Whether the characters in a telefeature are middle class or working class, the "problem" they confront is invariably posed as a social, rather than merely emotional, issue. Dialogue speaks to that issue and plot structure moves along a straight line that is drawn from the initial awareness of the problem to the crisis it engenders in the family to its solution. There is always less subtlety in the dramatic interactions of characters, less nuance in their gestures and dialogues because the purpose of the dramatic interactions is simply to reveal the roots of the problems in a more sociological than psychological way.

This is one of the reasons a film like *Ordinary People* appears to be "classier," more intelligent, or even more profound than it really is. In a TV movie about teen suicide, for example, each interaction, each bit of dialogue, will be informative and further the plot, whereas in *Ordinary People*, dialogue and interaction serve to illuminate in more subtle ways characters' psychological idiosyncrasies. In one of Conrad's sessions with his psychiatrist, for example, he relates an incident in which he is talking to someone and notices that "he kept tapping on his shoe and it was like his shoe would crack off." Having told this bit of observational trivia, he compares himself to a character in a TV family drama: "I kept thinking John Boy [of "The Waltons"] would have said something about the way he felt."

The entire film is composed of such little epiphanies, meant to imply rather than spell out monumentally profound insights into the human personality and character. The comparison with John

Boy is particularly revealing of the film's strategy. It is of course true that TV characters, in series like "The Waltons" as well as in TV movies, always say "something about the way [they feel]." Films like *Ordinary People* are more circumspect about such things. They honor the viewer with the assumption that she/he does not need things spelled out, that a word, a reference, a hand movement, will be clue enough to the deeper workings of the psyche that are the prime movers of the narrative. In this case, of course, the incident is meant to illustrate Conrad's feeling of being socially inept and inarticulate. This film pays a lot of attention to such moments of internal angst about fitting in, behaving appropriately. Beth does this to a fault; Conrad, who cannot achieve such "control," is treated sympathetically because he is therefore a more "real" person. Interior life is all here. In TV movies it counts for much less.

Another reason for this kind of exclusive focus on psychic trivia and tempest-in-a-teapot dramatic eruptions is that movies like *Ordinary People*, in a far more extreme way than TV movies, deny the existence of a relevant larger community, much less society. TV movies reduce social issues to family problems. Nonetheless, social issues do figure as their subject matter. They may address us all as members of families, as John Ellis astutely notes (1982, 165–67), but there is an implied corollary. Television envisions society as a collection of families, but society—however it is presumed to exist—does in fact exist. There is never a doubt, whether we are given statistics about the problem in the text or invited to a discussion or report about it afterwards, that we are being addressed as members of a social order being threatened by a disruptive force. Suicide is one such threat. A TV movie about suicide will fairly scream out "You are at risk here! Be on guard and know what to do." Very often, we will be informed about how likely we are to be hit by such a crisis and provided with other "documentary-style" pieces of information.

Films do not exist in the same kind of social space. In film, as Ellis has observed, "the position offered to the spectator is that of the seer who renders the film intelligible" (Ellis 1982, 83). In other words, the film spectator exists as an individual separate from the rest of society and free of identification with any social unit. His or her role is to privately read and inform the text with meaning. This role is as private and psychological as the experiences of the characters in *Ordinary People*.

In keeping with this distinction between the cinematic and televisual aparatuses is a parallel distinction between the conventions governing treatment of family matters. In a TV movie, the maintenance of the integrity of the family, the primary social unit from which the larger social structure is formed, is primary. In film, however, even middle-brow domestic drama like *Ordinary People*, it is the fate of the individual soul that matters. Thus, TV movies about family crises invariably end with the family made whole in some way. This is hardly the case in film. *Ordinary People* (like most TV movies about families) explicitly addresses the question of the breakdown of the family and poses solutions. Its solutions, however, are radically different. It finds a central family member—the mother, no less—wanting and does away with her. The two male survivors carry on in truncated but loving fashion. This conclusion seems more radical than it is. Divorce, emotional dysfunction, scandal, and tragedy are and long have been facts of life in America. The Jarretts are no more interesting or enlightening than one's own family or neighbors. The only thing vaguely startling about the film is its doing away with the mother, its portrayal of the male parent as the "real mother." Banishment of a family member occurs in TV movies only when murder is involved. Even sexual offenders are invariably reconstructed and reintegrated into the family. Moreover, it is quite rare for the villain to be the mother. Mothers are the key figures of TV families. But this aspect of current popular theatrical films too is part of the zeitgeist and a not particularly attractive part at that. The subtle (or not so subtle) sexism implied in the *Ordinary People* ending is a reflection of the broadly felt backlash against feminism so prevalent since the seventies. TV movies, corny and old-fashioned as they may be, never have—for their own contradictory reasons—engaged in that kind of woman baiting.

To see how TV movies handle this kind of domestic trauma, let us look at *Sarah T.*, an early example of the genre but one that holds up quite well. In fact, the only hints that it is an early telefeature come from such obvious details as clothing style—Sarah wears bell-bottom jeans, for example—and the fact that it begins with the kind of statistics common in the early days, when these films were presented as semidocumentaries as a way of diverting attention from their sensational subject matter. Right after the credits, we are told, for example, that "It takes fifteen years for an adult to become an alcoholic" but "only fifteen months for a teenager." Such information, in a more recent telefeature, would be provided later, in the discussions or news segments that pick up the theme. There is, by now, an established role for "issue" telefeatures that is understood to be a serious social one and is promoted as such.

Sarah T. starts much like Ordinary People. There is a large, lavishly decorated home that reeks of comfort and taste. There are a mother and a father, it seems. And there is a teenage girl in the midst of what we gradually come to understand is an emotional crisis. In this case, however, the father figure turns out to be a stepfather, while Sarah's real father, whom her mother has just divorced but to whom Sarah is deeply attached, is irresponsible and infantile. The crisis here is precipitated by the newly constructed family's move to a new community.

Like Conrad, Sarah has difficulty adjusting to her social circumstances and feels left out and lonely. Unlike Conrad, her problem and her way of handling it are emotionally straightforward and one-dimensional: she begins to drink. The key scenes in this drama are always emblematic in their didactic purpose. At a party given by her parents, for example, Sarah is ill at ease and begins to drain the cocktail glasses she clears and brings to the kitchen. The lesson to parents in the audience is clear: children learn from your example.

The next bit of pressure on Sarah comes, again, from her well-meaning but insensitive mother, who arranges a date for her with the most popular boy in school, whose father is a business associate of her husband's. Angry and terrified, Sarah drinks too much at the party to which her date takes her and finds it brings her out of her shell. She performs as a singer and impresses the boy and his friends. This is very different from the events in Ordinary People, where in a parallel party scene, Beth precipitates an outbreak of rage from Conrad when she not so subtly avoids being photographed with him. Everyone else ignores the incident, since the point is that these well-bred people choose not to acknowledge emotions or tensions. Conrad, having had months of therapy, breaks the rules of decorum and smashes the camera.

The lessons here are obviously very different. On television, we are instructed in how, within the confines of our homes, to handle a particular social problem affecting many young people. Understand this; do that; get help here and there. In *Ordinary People*, the message is always private and psychological. Get a good shrink; deal with your feelings. In a sense, *Ordinary People* preaches less middle-class respectability while *Sarah T.*, true to its role and its medium, preaches it more. It is the first "say no" TV message for teens and parents and is very much a social statement. *Ordinary People*, on the other hand, can almost be read—as is common in sophisticated Hollywood drama—as an asocial statement. Break the stifling rules of social convention, it says mildly. Let your feelings hang out no matter what the rest of the world thinks. And of course the ultimate message: break up a family if necessary.

Ordinary People is still, of course, an extremely conventional film and a very safe and conservative one too. The characters are wealthy and attractive, and the ending is comic rather than tragic in the sense that the villain is expunged and the hero is united with his father in love and harmony. When Hollywood ventures outside the realm of middle-class domestic drama to deal with political matters, the picture is rarely so sunny, especially the final picture. *Silkwood*, the story of union activist Karen Silkwood, is a clear example. It is not just that Karen Silkwood ends up isolated and then dead. It is also that her attempts to make positive changes in the public sphere are clearly and cynically presented as futile.

Sarah T. is radically different. The narrative continues predictably. Sarah's real father disappoints her. Her drinking gets out of hand and she loses her boyfriend. She is reduced to prostitution to pay for liquor, and finally she takes her ex-boyfriend's horse out on a drunken ride and the horse is killed. This is rock bottom, of course. Therapy and Alcoholics Anonymous follow. The good family is healed; the bad father is revealed to be a jerk. The roles of mother and father in this movie and in *Ordinary People* are, as we have noted, mirror images. In classic telefeature style, Sarah's mother sees her errors and changes, thus facilitating the happy ending—a sober Sarah and an intact nuclear family. If *Ordinary People* leaves us with a sense of unrecoverable loss, a certain sadness at a world transformed, of long-held beliefs and values unmasked and discarded, *Sarah T.* ends on no such note of sorrow or emotional damage. It is implicitly utopian in its suggestion that permanent ideals and forms can always be restored; that Eden is in fact the natural state of affairs. TV movies are about messages of hope and endurance. They are given that role in our society and perform it in the interest of commerce and political harmony but also—at least in part—in the interest of human dreams.

3
Feminist Theory and the TV Movie: What the Genre Does Best

How to make viewers and critics of dramatic narrative take the movie of the week seriously—that is the project of this book. I have been arguing against the grain of just about everyone who has bothered to comment publicly on the form. Even the *New York Times* TV critic John O'Connor, a man whose job requires that he find virtue in at least some of what he reviews, consistently, and ever so loftily, reviles the TV movie for its "undeveloped, stereotypical characters," its "oversimplification" (O'Connor 1983, C12), and other cardinal sins of the lit crit canon.

As we have already seen, these criticisms have more than a bit of merit. The movies we have looked at so far, whatever their virtues, have had more than their share of trashiness and sentimentality. Given the current critical interest among feminists in reevaluating both melodrama and soap opera, and the rich, rewarding work that has been done on these themes, however, there is at least a respectable tradition for making a case for the contradictory, but still in many ways positive, aspects of TV movies.

This chapter, in which I analyze what I believe to be the very best of the genre, the movies dealing with serious feminist issues, is a lot harder to write. For one thing, we are dealing less with melodrama than with classic social realism, a style not widely championed or even written about much in feminist or other current trend-setting schools of critical discourse. From semiotics to postmodernism to the new genre studies, the interest is in finding new hidden meanings in classic and mass media texts. Realism does not lend itself to that kind of thing. What you see is what you get. How boring. The second problem in defending these movies, as drama and as social statement, arises from the first. In melodramatic and sexually titillating movies, the politics is found between the lines or, perhaps more accurately, behind the frames. Whatever the limits or sins of the overall statement, there is still something deeply important, especially from an audience-response perspective, in demonstrating the subversive power of a form generally considered wholly reactionary. What women see and feel when they watch these shows is often liberatory, in spite of the soupy, socially respectable happy endings. With social realism, on the other hand, the glaringly contrived endings, the indulgence in sensation and tear jerking, and especially the misrepresentations of social and political reality, stand naked as Eve before the godlike critical gaze.

Nonetheless, these are the films that most excite and move me, for a whole lot of not-so-fashionable reasons that, I think, have long been due for rethinking. With all their social and artistic limitations and sins, they manage to engage a mass audience of millions in issues presented by the news media from an abstract, bloodless perspective.

As for Hollywood, it rarely treats the kinds of themes that are standard fare for TV movies at all. When have you seen theatrical features on the plight of women clerical or factory workers, of sexually harassed women, of lesbians fighting for the custody of children? Once in a blue moon. It is just not good box office. But all these themes, and scores more, have been done on TV and watched by millions. Obviously, this does not counter the critical complaints about the way these films are done. If they were really as dumb as the critics say, they would do more harm than good. But at least a large percentage of them are not. True, for reasons we have already discussed, the artistic conventions of the form make for a far less sophisticated treatment of life than theatricals can present. There is not a lot of emotional subtlety, only rare efforts at atmospheric nuance, and always a lowest-common-denominator insistence on spelling out each step of the story lest the least sophisticated viewer get confused or, worse yet, switch channels looking for more action.

TV movies are limited, as we have seen, by the need to place every issue in the context of an idealized model of the nuclear family. As I have argued elsewhere (Rapping 1985, 10–14), the role of TV movies—for economic and social reasons—is to domesticate social issues, to personalize them and to push a view of problem resolution that is profamily in the most reactionary, sledge-hammer-like way. When families do break up, it is because they were "bad" families. The heroine is implicitly or explicitly moving toward a new, "good" family—the only really happy ending for women. Even movies that portray households more truly reflective of current realities—single mothers, gay couples—force their protagonists into a model of family dynamics that would make Ward and June Cleaver feel right at home. *The Ryan White Story*, for example, about a mother coping with a young son who has AIDS, made the single parent into a combination of mother and father without ever suggesting any of the problems associated with the superwoman syndrome. Mrs. White was just doing her motherly duty. The absence of a husband was not an issue.

Whatever the implicit critique of family norms informing TV movies about incest, wife abuse, teen unrest, and so on, this ultimate idealization and resurrection of a "good" family, upon which each narrative turns, undercuts and negates that critique. As those who have been restudying Hollywood family melodrama have often and persuasively demonstrated, the theatrical family drama does the opposite. It presents the very dynamics TV movies therapeutically "fix" as unfixable, hopelessly unworkable, malignant with decadence and emotional vampirism. Thomas Schatz, in his study of Hollywood melodrama, has described its presentation of traditional family life well. The ideal of the family "as a 'natural' as well as social collective, a self-contained society in and of itself," he argues, is always undercut by its placement of that family "within a highly structured socioeconomic milieu," one in which "family roles are determined by the larger social community." Because this milieu is represented by an "American small town committed to fading values and mores (and) representing an extended but perverted family in which human elements (love, honesty, generosity, interpersonal contact) have either solidified into repressive social conventions or disappeared altogether" (Schatz 1981, 225), these films unmask the myth of middle-class family harmony and reveal the social reaction and personal tragedy it fosters. The Hollywood melodrama, then, is a dark tragedy of the breakdown of the family, a view of family life that proves that all the king's horses and all the king's men cannot possibly revive it or make it work. This dark drama is obviously not the stuff of the sunny TV movie, where bad fathers reform or are replaced by good ones and the family goes on to furnish ever more comfy living rooms cleaned with ever more elaborate and expensive gadgets, gums, and goos—all to be bought by the heroine and her counterpart in the home audience. The message of the commercials is the message of the movies: it has to be or sponsors will bolt. No wonder critics find the movies easy to disdain.

The contrast between melodrama and social realism (which, in television, actually becomes social/commercial realism), is at the heart of the other problem in defending and appreciating TV movies. For all their "just the facts ma'am" simplicity, they retain important elements of melodrama. They deal in passion, heartbreak, rage, histrionics. They are melodramatic in their excessive, often manipulative, play on emotions. But they lack those darker, more complicated qualities that characterize the Hollywood movie. Melodrama, according to Christine Gledhill, typically "attests to forces, desires, fears which . . . appear to operate in human life independent of rational explanation" (Gledhill 1987, 31). Even, perhaps most strongly, when melodrama is most "unrealistic," it suggests recognizable depths of the human spirit that ring true on some level and that defy the language and scope of mere reason, of social, legal, or even psychological "management." This is just what social issue TV movies, no matter how flagrantly they borrow from the conventions of melodrama, cannot do. By their very artistic nature, and by virtue of their social and economic function on commercial TV, they must insist on rational explanation, whether psychological or sociological. Like their Hollywood siblings, their subject and project is to delve into the pathologies of families, but they do this in ploddingly and transparently understandable ways. Rational explanations and therapeutic resolutions of family madnesses are their stock-in-trade.

Here is where the critical problem lies: TV movies borrow from melodrama but apply its conventions to matters more accurately termed sentimental. They are obliged to appeal to sentiment and emotion, to make us cry in sympathy or cringe in horror. These techniques are obviously taken from the highest of high melodrama. But, taken out of generic context, placed in a world where the darker mysteries and tragic endings of melodrama are taboo, they seem particularly soppy and manipulative. Where suicide, prison, financial ruin, abandonment, and isolation are common and inevitable endings to high melodrama, TV movies get their gasps, their tears, their heart-stopping suspense from much easier, more sentimental themes. The graduation of a kid who had been on the streets and heading for jail, the trophy won by a kid with Down's syndrome in the Special Olympics, the triumph of a middle-aged man who learns to read, this is the stuff of TV movies. What comes first—the heartbreak of parents, the passion of a special teacher, social worker, or doctor, the predictable intermediate failures and relapses—is one dimensional and simplistically presented. There is no fascinating subtext to these stories. There is no way for the subtle viewer to smile knowingly at the ironic contrast between form and substance, between what appears to be happy family life and what lurks below the surface. This is the crux of the critical disdain for the form—disdain that in my opinion is elitist and misguided. Avant-garde critics have scorned sheer, easy pleasure in art, have insisted on art's role as distancer from feeling so that audiences may dwell rationally on the work, for too long. In an essay on the overwhelmingly positive response of West German viewers to the critically and politically disdained American miniseries *Holocaust*, Andreas Huyssen takes on this position and asks, "Why are emotions trivial? Who says?" (Huyssen 1986, 95). Who indeed? The fact is that emotion is a crucial element in one's coming to understand, and certainly to be involved with, the problems of society. The TV movie's need for hooks, for sensation, for emotional fireworks serve many not-so-noble ends, to be sure. But sometimes—and the movies we are about to look at are prime examples—they serve progressive, albeit (need we say once more?) limited and contradictory, ends as well.

From Ordinary to Extraordinary:
Some Working-Class Heroines

The Burning Bed, a TV movie about Francine Hughes, a battered wife acquitted of killing her husband, was first broadcast in October 1984. It drew an estimated 75 million viewers and is the fourth-highest-rated TV movie ever shown. A year later, in October 1985, *Silent Witness*, about a young woman who, with her husband, watches her brother-in-law and two other men rape a woman in a local bar and is finally moved to defy her family and testify in court, was not a blockbuster. Still, it won a respectable Nielsen rating and was seen by approximately 47 million people, hardly an insignificant number. Both features have been rerun and are available on videocassette, making the total viewership, while undocumented, much greater.

The huge audiences for these features is even more impressive when one considers their tone and substance. These are grim, downbeat stories, stories that, if they were presented in theaters, would almost surely have short runs and lose money. Yet they were shown on television and drew huge audiences.

The success of these TV movies—both of a high quality of seriousness and artistic execution—can be understood in part by referring back to the way the medium functions.

As we have seen, TV producers and sponsors often play a game of negotiation that involves the strange intermingling of incompatible value systems. Sensation draws audiences. Stars draw sponsors. Anyone who wants to produce serious, much less socially relevant, TV drama must start from those facts. Sexual violence is nothing if not sensational. Having Farrah Fawcett and Valerie Bertinelli—both big, popular names—as stars sweetened the pot. But the substance of the films actually had little to do with either sensation or glamour. Far from it. These were message movies of a very old-fashioned kind. And while they both moved inexorably toward the obligatory "happy ending, nice and tidy," to use some words from Brecht, and managed, along the way, to distort a lot of social and political realities, they were, in their own quiet, contradictory ways, more than somewhat subversive of existing attitudes about sex, marriage, and the family. They were

69

also—and this was clearly an element of their subversive power—intensely moving.

That these two films stand a notch above most, both socially and artistically, has a lot to do with their producer, Robert Greenwald, who also directed *The Burning Bed*. These are only two of an impressive list of similar features—many on feminist themes—that Greenwald's independent production company has successfully sold to networks and audiences. Coming out of a New York theater background—off-off-Broadway at that—Greenwald went to Los Angeles to make films. He found that TV was far more receptive to his kind of social issue drama than the movie studios (he told me in 1985 in an unpublished interview). Greenwald's idealism was not, however, what made him successful. It was his business savvy, his understanding of how the game worked and how he had to play it to be able to do the kinds of things he wanted to do. He did what he considers "a lot of trash" while he was learning the ropes and plotting his strategy. When he finally set up his own company he was already hot. He had credibility and a reputation for delivering. The success of *The Burning Bed* made him even hotter. It demonstrates the subtle mix of slick and serious, in just the right balance, that can and sometimes does make for high-quality TV.

Greenwald's style and strategy, evident in both *The Burning Bed* and *Silent Witness*, are unusual. Their success has paved the way for other interesting producers. For one thing, both stories feature working-class characters in working-class settings. Greenwald has never, he says, worked on a soundstage. He sometimes scouts for locations for weeks. He likes the feel of gritty reality, not pretty fantasy. In the context of commercial TV as experienced by viewers, there is a problem with this kind of unglamorous, unflattering portrayal of working-class life that we will consider later in the chapter. Looking only at video aesthetics, however, Greenwald's brand of video vérité is remarkably powerful and effective.

The Burning Bed, the better of the two films, is also structurally unusual. Whereas almost all TV drama presents events in strict chronological order, this one uses flashbacks. The story is framed by opening, closing, and intermittent returns to scenes of Fran, the heroine, in prison conferring with her lawyer after she has

killed her husband. As the drama progresses, past and present begin to converge until, at movie's end, when the trial and verdict
are shown, we have been brought up to date. This is hardly a
sophisticated structural strategy when compared to theatrical
films. *Last Year at Marienbad* it is not. Even popular courtroom
suspense films like *The Jagged Edge* use more complex techniques. The point is that television does not. Network executives
and sponsors actually operate on the basis of some very insulting
assumptions about their audiences. They are cautious to a fault
and prefer simple, even stupid, to anything novel. In that context
The Burning Bed becomes even more interesting.

This is not to overstate the case. An overview of the dramatic
developments within the context of the framing flashbacks reveals a typically oversimplified telling of a sensational tale. For example, Greenwald uses the standard device of beginning each
segment with a specific date. Having been introduced to Fran and
her court-appointed lawyer in prison, having seen her bruised,
bedraggled, and psychologically beaten down to the point where
she cannot, or will not, speak, we finally hear her utter her first
words, begin to tell her story. The scene then shifts to 1963, and
we hear Fran's voice-over narration as we see her initial meeting
with her future husband.

That first segment, from 1963, contains eight brief scenes
chronicling the courtship and ends with the doomed and dreary
wedding. Fran is attracted to Mickey Hughes, with his James Dean
slouch and his "kind of wild" reputation, for obvious reasons.
She is shy; he is apparently smooth. She is innocent; he is apparently worldly and experienced. She thinks little of herself; he apparently thinks she is terrific. It is an old story, filled on one level
with sociological and psychological cliché. On another level,
though, it is moving and informative, for all its obviousness. What
it lacks in intellectual and emotional complexity it makes up for
in visual and dramatic power.

To relate the plot does not capture the texture of the film, the
sources of its impact. The scenes mark key points in her often
reluctant agreement to marry him. He wants sex; she holds out,
sixties "good-girl" style, until he begs for marriage. She—as is
typical in these movies—has a best friend who sees the handwrit-
ing on the tract house wall but is not able to dissuade Fran from

71

marriage. As for Fran, she is no passive neurotic. She has real doubts about being tied down and a strong desire to make something of herself, to be independent. Dreams of romance and togetherness understandably win out in this preliberation, working-class world. The segment ends, however, with two events presented as blatantly, unmistakably—to even the youngest or least sophisticated viewer—ominous. Mickey takes money from his mother to buy the ring and, catastrophically, they move in with his parents because he has no job. Nothing violent, or even vaguely sensational, has yet happened. Still, the performances, the setting, and the televisual apparatus combine to keep viewers riveted. A sense of claustrophobia, of poisonously twisted family dynamics, is already evident and frightening in these scenes. The interiors are small, close, and ugly, in a style only poverty seems to breed. The Hughes house is not pleasant enough to provide relief from the family problems. It is not big enough to contain the submerged hostilities and deceptions it breeds. In a later segment, the issue of personal aesthetics is spelled out. Fran buys a frilly blouse for a dollar at Kmart. Mickey, obsessively jealous and possessive, rips it off and hits her, for the first time. The elder Hugheses, placed in the midst of the conflict, choose to ignore it and leave the room.

On one level, of course, this is mere sociology, what every feminist supposedly knows. But as visual drama it is much more than that. The interpersonal tensions are palpable here, and they are scary in a way that no theoretical study of woman battering can be. Fran's economic problems, her training in "womanly virtue," her inability to understand what is happening, are visually and emotionally concrete here.

The limits of television, the need to keep things in close quarters, to deal largely in close-ups and one-on-one interchanges, are here made to work for the director. The faces of the principals, Paul LeMat and Farrah Fawcett, become embedded in our memories as a result of the intensity of what they express in such limited scenes and sets. The lack of glamour in this production is also remarkable for television. In this movie, Fawcett is about as frumpy as a major star has ever allowed herself to be. As it proceeds, she looks worse and worse. Her hair is straggly and dirty, her clothes mere rags, her bruises—internal and external—

glaringly apparent. When the violence finally begins, and then, inexorably, escalates, we are more than prepared for it. Far from sensationalizing it, the film makes it seem as tawdry, as painful, as unheroic as it really is. That it is the late scenes of physical abuse that NBC chose to use in its teaser clips promoting the movie is understandable. Such are the contradictions of television. The viewer, however, waits a long time to see these scenes and, in context, they are far from titillating. On the contrary, Greenwald uses some sophisticated video techniques to create the sense of family pathology and misery. We often hear the voices of the children as they watch their father hurt their mother. At other times we hear the sounds of battle while we watch the terrified children. In these scenes it is as though the house shakes and quakes in sync with the breakdown of the family it contains.

It is not only technique, but also the interplay of ideology and technique, that makes this movie so powerful. In the second framing interview between Fran and her lawyer, for example, a political motif is introduced. The attorney shows Fran some letters she has received from other battered women who were inspired by Fran's story to leave their husbands. When the second narrative sequence begins, this positive political note is countered by the introduction of the first of a long series of scenes in which the power of the major social institutions—from the family to the social service bureaucracy to the criminal justice system—is dramatically shown to encourage and foster domestic violence, to make it very difficult for women to escape.

After Mickey's first act of violence Fran goes home to her mother, who sends her back where she "belongs." "Women have to put up with their men," she tells her daughter. "If you make a hard bed you have to lay in it." Finding herself pregnant, and Mickey more and more indolent and aggressive, Fran turns to social service agencies that offer no real help. By 1970, now the mother of three, Fran does leave. Again, the power of family dogma brings her back. Her in-laws refuse to acknowledge that there is such a thing as divorce, for example. "It ain't no divorce," says her mother-in-law. "Mickey loves you." Mickey, for his part, falls apart, has a car accident, and is laid up for months. Fran's guilt brings her back, "temporarily," since he will allow no one else to nurse him.

When she leaves again, he takes the children. Again the state offers no help and again she returns. This time she is determined to better herself by attending business school. Mickey is more and more threatened and out of control. He destroys her books and virtually rapes her, and—that night—she sets his bed on fire, takes her kids, and runs.

I relate this plot development in detail because it points up the way in which a rich portrayal of all-too-typical institutional beliefs and behaviors, in the family and out, fuels the growing desperation, isolation, and ultimate violence of its emblematic heroine. Greenwald is very good at painting Fran into a corner, visually, dramatically, and ideologically. Her acquittal, on grounds of temporary insanity, reflects the power of the film's multilevel argument. The problem is painfully, gruesomely spelled out in all its emotional and social complexity. But there is also an underlying feminist message here: Fran is right and the world is wrong. Fran is ultimately vindicated and valorized, on feminist grounds.

The down side of this clearly superior movie is that it diminishes, distorts, and omits a lot. First, like all TV drama, it lacks a larger political, historical context for its subject. The actual Fran Hughes case, for example, was taken up by feminist organizations that played a major role in developing the legal strategy and in publicizing the case and raising money for Hughes's defense. The movie, steeped in convention, invents a male attorney to act as the heroine's sole savior. Greenwald, for his part, insists that there were technical reasons for not including the women's movement in the film. "We couldn't figure out a way to make it work," he says. "The form isn't suited to scenes of mass demonstrations and that kind of thing."

Well, yes and no. On the one hand there is no reason at all why TV cannot show mass activity. The news does it all the time. On the other hand, what Greenwald is really saying is that the conventions of the TV movie, conventions developed to fit the needs of sponsors and the larger social biases of commercial television, do not allow for other than personal, individual solutions, even to social problems.

Greenwald's—and most other producers'—insistence on the apolitical nature of their decisions, their sole concern with "what works" dramatically, points up one of the biggest contradictions of network television. I have no doubt of the sincerity of these statements. Nonetheless, it is a truism of media theory that "acculturation," the learned, internalized methods and criteria of people who work in the field, plays a big part in keeping controversy out of media of all kinds. People tend to adopt the beliefs and values of those they work with.

For journalists these are usually the important figures in a given beat. A reporter travels with, drinks with, socializes with, the very people she or he is supposed to report on impartially. Moving out of the circle, writing things that contradict its view of itself—in a broad philosophical sense—is professional suicide. For TV producers the problem is similar. Television, as we have seen, systematically focuses our attention on family and personal life. It refuses to place dramatic narrative in a broad social or historic context. It insists, rather, that problems—even widespread social problems like domestic violence—be viewed, understood, and tackled only in terms of isolated cases and within the limits of existing social agencies. Most importantly, perhaps, from a sponsor's perspective, it demands solutions that reinforce middle-class values.

If feminism were seen as the agent of Fran Hughes's acquittal, the message would have been very different. The movie would have suggested that poor, powerless people could band together to effect changes in the existing social order. It did not do that. Instead, it suggested that a good lawyer, in a well-cut suit, someone who implicitly comes from the domestic and professional environment represented by sponsors and network executives, was all Hughes needed. Although there was no romantic aspect to this client/lawyer relationship, symbolically it was, nonetheless, a kind of Cinderella story. Fran trusts her lawyer; he gets her off; she returns to business school to join his world, moving on up, presumably, to the kind of setting we see in every commercial during the broadcast.

This brings us to the question of class and network TV. Greenwald's consistent interest in the dignity and drama of working-class life is remarkable and commendable. Still, there is a subtext to his movies that emerges most clearly in the contrast between ads and drama. Fran wears Kmart schlock; the women selling household cleaners in the ads that work in counterpoint to her story wear expensive, perfectly tailored outfits, even when they are cleaning. Fran's hair is a mess; theirs is professionally coiffed and in perfect order, even as they supposedly mop the floor.

The implication here is subtle but problematic: people who live in shabby tract houses, who have no style, who lack education or professional work, are likely candidates for the most sordid of crimes. The marvelous realism of the violence in the film is double-edged. We see the violence in all its brutal nastiness in a way that middle-class dramas of family pathology dare not portray. The incestuous father in *Something About Amelia*, for instance, is never seen in his worst moments. He is never out of control, drunk, or brutally abusive, at least to the camera's eye. It is all very low key and suggestive. Where Mickey Hughes is seen as the ultimate slob and beast, his middle-class counterpart is always rational, well groomed, mannered. He ends up not dead but cured and forgiven. There is more than a hint here that middle-class professionals, educated and wealthy, are somehow inherently less bestial, more worthy of forgiveness and redemption. Joel Steinberg notwithstanding, this view of class difference is pervasive on TV and is informed, unquestionably, by a need to play to the paying audience.

Sisterhood Lives, Almost

Silent Witness, another tale of working-class male bestiality and female victimization and ultimate heroism, is a bit different. For one thing, the heroine, Anna, is not the victim but the sister-in-law of the perpetrator. Her heroism—and this is really impressive—is not in her own self-interest but in the interest of justice and a movingly spelled out sense of sisterhood, if not as a general principle, at least between two women, Anna and the rape victim, Patti.

While this movie lacks the emotional and visual rawness and impact of *Burning Bed*, its focus on an "activist" (in the broadest sense of the term) heroine is actually more advanced politically. Inspired, like *Burning Bed*, by a real incident—the gang rape of a young woman in a working-class bar in Massachusetts—the movie uses this incident only as a starting point (and, certainly, a selling point to sensation-hungry sponsors and network executives). The almost universal tendency to diverge from fact, to fictionalize TV movies in large and small ways, is determined by a few factors. Sometimes rights to life stories cannot be obtained. More often, though, it is just television's odd brand of poetic license. What "works" on television is defined by the conventions of the form, which are themselves determined by what sponsors and networks think will sell. "Social significance with a lifted face" is how Todd Gitlin describes the social issue TV movie. Networks like "little personal stories [they] think a mass audience will take as revelations of the contemporary" (Gitlin 1984, 163), he says. In *Silent Witness*, as in *Burning Bed*, this means couching the story in family rather than political terms.

Gitlin's cynicism is perhaps overstated, as is his sense of the underlying politics of these films. Politics is central to these movies, all the more so because it is literally left out of the picture. To personalize a political issue is after all to present an implicit, but still powerful, political position. It is to state loudly and clearly that larger political issues and perspectives do not figure in these matters. Since they obviously do, there is a subtext in television's established conventions that can only be seen as reactionary and misleading. On the other hand, in the case of these two Greenwald movies (and it is interesting that of all the writers and directors Gitlin quotes, all the progressive programs he analyzes in his much-acclaimed and influential book, he totally ignores Greenwald's more serious contributions), the use of family themes is not just heart-warming or familiar. It is very obviously a way of critiquing family dynamics. Happy endings and sentimentality notwithstanding, these dramas present suprisingly rich analyses of what is wrong with traditional family ideology and dynamics, from a feminist perspective, in ways that are certainly politically meaningful and provocative.

Had *Silent Witness* focused on the rape victim, it might have been equally effective but would have been very different in its message. Movies about victims fighting back—*A Case of Rape, A Matter of Sex, Fun and Games*, and of course *The Burning Bed*, to name a few—are far more common than films about moral action on behalf of others. When such themes are featured in TV movies, the hero is almost always male. Theatrical film and TV

77

drama are full of male heroes standing up for what is right, from
High Noon to "Lou Grant." That is part of our traditional stereo-
type of masculinity. Not so femininity. To see a young working-
class woman, a supermarket checkout clerk, transform herself
from a typically passive, uninvolved, and unsophisticated girl absorbed wholly in her marriage and family into someone who
sacrifices everything—her husband, her job, her reputation—for
what she believes in is remarkable enough to deserve notice.

There is nothing glamorous about Anna Dunne. Her home is as
plain and drab as the Hughes home. Her family—actually her husband's family—is as unwittingly vicious and repressive as the
Hughes family. They believe in family loyalty, in sticking together
as a clan. They pressure Anna to betray her own values or be os-
tracized. Even their strategy for discrediting Anna on the witness
stand is loaded with sexist significance. Anna, it turns out, is infer-
tile, while her sister-in-law, the rapist's wife, is anything but. In
the dirty laundry that gets aired in court, we learn that Anna's husband once was unfaithful for reasons connected with his feeling
inadequate in not being able to produce a child. Motherhood,
family loyalty even when family behavior is immoral or criminal,
standing by your man, all these figure—as they did in *Burning
Bed*—in Anna's story and serve to explain the enormous hostility
and cruelty with which she is treated.

Anna is not Fran Hughes, though. She may be as innocent and
unworldly, but she finally acts not on instinct, for animal survival,
but intelligently, consciously, and for abstract reasons. The way
her transformation comes about is very much like that in the
other movie. The first half of the film charts, in pointedly sociological and psychological scenes, the various family and personal
pressures that keep her silent. She is afraid to get involved, as
most of us are. She loves her husband and has a good marriage.
She is part of a working-class family and community that define
her life, give her security.

The turning point comes when she visits Patti, the victim, and
they share high school memories, girl talk, and personal experiences. Patti, it turns out, is an alcoholic, an AA member who,
on the night of her rape, went on a binge. Again, televisual limits
create powerful drama. The threadbare little boardinghouse
room in which they meet creates a strong sense of the loneliness

and deprivation of Patti's life, to which Anna responds sympathetically. They joke about Anna's husband Kevin's job, collecting garbage. Anna is moved by Patti's story. Finally they embrace before parting. When Patti—encouraged by her therapy group to press charges as an act of personal empowerment—is humiliated and emotionally destroyed by the defense and commits suicide, Anna feels a responsibility that leads her to separate from her husband and testify in court. The dirty tricks played on her after this, by her mother-in-law, her sister-in-law (who refuses to believe in her husband's guilt because she cannot afford to end her marriage and support her two children alone), and an old boyfriend paid to seduce and betray her, are standard TV melodrama. They are also, however, very real pictures of the lengths to which families and the legal system will go to preserve what can only be seen as patriarchal and sexist values.

All the criticisms of *Burning Bed* apply here as well. There is no male lawyer to save Patti, but there are two representatives of the legal system committed to justice who endlessly pressure Anna. The system does work after all, at least in individual cases involving exemplary individuals. Patti is sacrificed but Anna's marriage, ultimately, is reconstructed and saved. Kevin sees the light, defies his family, and reunites with Anna. He even testifies himself.

In focusing on Anna and on her realization of her bond with victims of sexual aggression and her responsibility to act, this movie, in its dramatically unexceptional way, takes a real political stand. That she is reunited with her husband, that her ordinary working-class marriage is saved, may seem to contradict what I have said about class and TV movies. Kevin is not a brute. He is a man who can respect and love a woman as strong and independent as Anna. Actually, however, this movie too presents working-class family life, even "good" family life, as different from its middle-class counterpart.

Anna returns to a life far more limited than she clearly deserves. Having done what she has done, become who she has become, she seems unlikely to live happily ever after bagging groceries. In *A Matter of Sex*, the story of a group of female bank employees who strike for higher wages and better treatment, the one young woman who is transformed, as Anna has been, by her experience ends with a broken marriage and goes on to a career as a union organizer. That, it seems to me, is the far more likely ending to *Silent Witness*. In *Lois Gibbs and the Love Canal*, also made by Greenwald, the housewife heroine turned activist against toxic waste also loses her husband and goes on to organize. That Anna does not in any way change her life as a result of her experiences is unbelievable. But for working-class heroines—those few TV allows—it is an either/or situation. Keep the man or continue to grow and change.

Fran Hughes "lost" her husband. When, as in *Silent Witness*, the marriage is saved, the issues and actions addressed by the film are treated, more than usually, as isolated events, suspended in time, with no sense of future ramifications. With middle-class heroines it is different. From *Amelia Earhart* to the myriad mother/heroines of the family-in-trouble genre, they almost always get to have both work and man these days. Feminism, then, is seen by TV as a middle-class matter. In fact, since it has been accepted as a fact of life by the media, "Feminism" as the media likes to portray it is almost written across the screen of many of these movies. But between the lines and frames there is a qualification: for middle-class women only. And so, while Anna is quintessentially feminist in her behavior, far more so than most TV movie protagonists, the film overall denies that. Again we have a subtle class bias here.

The Female Gaze

One of the most profound insights of feminist film theory has been the realization that film traditionally assumes a "male gaze," that the implied audience is the male moviegoer who is assumed to identify with the male hero and to view the female protagonist as object, not subject. The importance of this realization cannot be overstated. It means that women viewers have been placed in a compromising position. They are seduced into identifying with the male point of view, the male protagonist. And yet, being women, they also identify, in obviously complicated ways, with the woman-as-object. Much of feminist film discourse has been taken up with this issue and how to resolve it. Should women opt out of the mainstream and produce independent films by and for women about their own experiences? Should they work within these conventions and try to subvert them? Or should they look more closely at the experience of the woman viewer and find, perhaps, ways that women have already and always "negotiated" their readings of male-oriented films in feminist ways?

In the recent rereadings of forties and fifties women's melodrama I quoted earlier, much of the debate centers on spectator response, on the actual message and effect women took away from these films. Laura Mulvey, in the forefront of this discourse, wrote in 1977 that "the few Hollywood films made with a female audience in mind evoke contradiction rather than reconciliation" with "society's overt pressures" (Mulvey 1977, 418). Other feminists have gone on to argue with Mulvey and find more "progressive" meanings in the genre. Linda Williams, for example, finds *Stella Dallas*—a film about a poor woman who sacrifices herself to ensure her daughter's happiness and then, when the daughter marries into wealth and position, is excluded from sharing the happiness she made possible—"progressive." Why? Because the film, in constructing "its spectator in a female subject position locked into a primary identification with another female subject" makes it possible for this spectator to impose her own radical feminist reading on the film (Williams 1984, 21).

These theories and debates have been inestimably valuable in helping us to see the complex and ambiguous issues involved in interpreting a film's meaning or effect. Whether negative in their view of the effects of family melodrama on women viewers or positive in their arguments for an ultimately "progressive" effect, these studies all have one thing in common: they understand that Hollywood, as an institution, produced films that at least on one important level reproduced the ideology that kept women trapped in patriarchal roles and self-images. Even those theories based on the belief—a belief I share—that the spectator has at least a limited ability to read films according to her own agenda acknowledge that this reading against the grain, as it were, implicitly assumes a level of sophistication and autonomy on the part of female spectators in the 1940s and 1950s that is complex and difficult to generalize.

I introduce this discussion of reader response theory and its various uses in interpreting the classic woman's film because it raises the question of a target audience, a matter that is key to any realistic reading of the movies we are analyzing and of the effect of movies targeted toward women on their chosen audience. It allows for a reading of the TV movies we have been discussing as, in certain important ways, more progressive and less ambiguous than the Hollywood melodramas now receiving so much critical attention. Artistically, they may be less interesting, but there is no denying their woman-focused approach to the very issues addressed in films like *Stella Dallas*. Certainly, as in the earlier films, we have to contend with institutionally programmed contradictions. But, it seems to me, it is easier to make a case for the (limited) progressive impact of these movies than for the Hollywood melodrama simply because they are so much less complex and convoluted in their presentations. They are so very simple and obvious, as their critics endlessly claim, that what is progressive about them is unmistakable to everyone watching.

To understand why a commercial, government-regulated form like television would present so many more or less progressive women's features, we need to look, once more, at television as institution. The fact is that television, far more than Hollywood, has always geared a hefty percentage of its product to an assumed female audience. If theatrical films almost universally assume a male gaze, and in rare cases where a female gaze is assumed provide narratives that are at best ambiguous, television as often as not assumes a female gaze and provides it with far more upbeat dramatic treatments of women's issues. The reasons in both cases are economic. Couples attend movies and—even today—men buy most of the tickets. Decisions about what to see are also assumed to be made primarily by the male. Television is different. Women, after all, are the primary shoppers. Sponsors, selling commodities, not movies, tend to play to that paying audience. Even though, as David Morley's fascinating studies of British family viewing habits show (Morley 1987), the man of the house tends to control the program selection process, women do watch television alone far more often than they go to movie houses. Most family homes today have more than one TV, and the rise of the VCR has made solo viewing even easier. The very fact that at least half of the made-for-TV movies are about women's issues is, after all, surprising and significant enough to have led me to write this book. In terms of feminist film and media theory, the fact that these movies assume a female gaze is a particularly important and overlooked fact.

The movies we have been analyzing in this chapter, about sexist crimes against women, are particularly impressive examples of what television can do right. We have already seen how many themes presented from a female perspective in TV movies are treated very differently in theatricals. With violent crimes against women, the contrast is even more dramatic. Rape and woman battering are—it is fair to say—almost never treated as political or even social issues in theatrical films. On the contrary, they are typically, and endlessly, presented as "normal" occurrences in films that deal with violence and crime.

When, in *The Godfather*, Michael Corleone punches his wife, upon learning she has had an abortion, there is no hint that this act constitutes wife abuse, a widespread, socially pathological crime. And from there the examples get worse and worse. How many films have you seen in which women are brutalized, raped, sexually demeaned? Hundreds. How many have in any way presented this sordid material from the victim's point of view? It is hard to name one. These actions always seem to play, in the more serious films like *Godfather*, as just one more symbol of the corruption and decadence of the hero and the social world he inhabits. In nonserious films, of course, they are simply part of the sleazy world of exploitation movies generally.

Seen in this perspective, movies like *Burning Bed* and *Silent Witness* seem all the more politically remarkable. From start to finish, no matter what their other flaws, they put the viewer solidly in the heroine's shoes and show her experiences as she lives and understands them. All other characters are secondary.

It is Fran and Anna we are made to identify with, not their husbands, their kids, or the values of the social institutions within which they act. It may be contradictory and problematic that these women are vindicated and triumph over their enemies; that they go on to live "better" lives; that the rest of the characters are made to come around to the woman's view or go down to defeat, humiliation, and worse. Nonetheless, from the perspective of the female audience, these movies provide something most mass media—or high art for that matter—deny them: a view of women as important, commendable, even remarkable people. These movies care about women's problems and treat them with dignity and respect.

Perhaps most heartening, even heartwarming—to legitimize, once more, a sentimental effect—they portray women as strong and independent, sisterly and supportive to each other. The device of the best friend/confidante may be contrived and by now overdone, but what genre convention is not? Is the buddy film, even at its most sophisticated—*Midnight Cowboy* or *Repo Man*, perhaps—or the lone hero fighting for justice or the redemption of his compromised soul—in films like *Prince of the City* or the original *Mad Max*—any less contrived or stereotypical? And yet these films, like the classic women's melodrama, are increasingly taken seriously by media critics and scholars, their conventions respected as TV movies, especially the ones about women, are not. This is a serious oversight and error.

To illustrate why, I will conclude this chapter with comparisons of our two TV movies and two similar theatricals, one from the 1940s, one recent. *Mildred Pierce*, a powerful 1945 melodrama, resembles *The Burning Bed* in several interesting ways. Structurally, it begins with the heroine being brought to jail, having confessed to killing her husband, who has been having an affair with her daughter. The daughter has actually committed the crime, but Mildred, a sacrificing mother in the Stella Dallas mold, prefers to take the blame herself and save her child. As in *Burning Bed*, then, we have a mother in jail for protecting her children. And as in *Burning Bed*, we get the real story in flashbacks told by the woman in voice-over narrative as she sits in jail. Finally, as in *Burning Bed*, we have a woman whose ultimately tragic relationships with men are presented at least in part as a result of the heroine's ambition to better herself, to provide a better life for her children.

The similarities end here. Mildred is not a sympathetic character. As Ann Kaplan puts it, this film helped "set the pattern for fifties and later films in [its] portrayal of the alternately masochistic and sadistic Mother" (Kaplan 1987, 134). Mildred, you see, was one of those "unnatural" creatures who was not satisfied with her role as wife to a nice but unexceptional man. We see her claw her way to the top of the business world as she moves from waitress to entrepreneur. In the process, her first marriage ends unhappily and her second, to a sexy ne'er-do-well who uses and humiliates her, ends in tragedy.

Ambition and sexual appetite are the characteristics that make Mildred seem a monster, a cold, ruthless bitch. And yet through it all, like Stella Dallas, she is obsessed with providing her daughter with a life of luxury, free of the hardship she herself experienced. The contradictions here are apparent, as is the creepy view of unconventional women. It is not farfetched to surmise that women viewers of the time, at least those already secretly feeling the strains of "the feminine mystique," could probably identify in some respects with Mildred, with her strength, her passion, her desire to escape boredom and mediocrity. But the message of this film noir was clear: the wages of rebellion, for women, are tragedy, loss, even prison or death.

Fran Hughes's story is told very differently, in a way that film— certainly in the forties and even now—has rarely embraced. Her desire to better herself, to escape the trap of what is presented as an all-too-"normal" kind of marriage, is justified. Her love of her children in no way conflicts with her desire to improve her own life. On the contrary, she acts as a mother in killing her husband. There is no ambiguity about Fran's character, no sense of "unnaturalness" even in her shockingly violent action. And while a male deus ex machina saves her, he is presented, at least, as fully in sympathy with her. This movie's female gaze and its progressive aspects are easy to recognize. Except for those women who, like Fran's mother and mother-in-law, accept and live by patriarchal dogma, it is hard to imagine a woman—especially one who has been abused—not identifying with Fran's plight and feeling happy about her legal victory.

Even in recent theatrical films, the situation is not quite so encouraging. In fact, *The Accused*, a box office hit released in the fall of 1988 and based on the same rape that inspired *Silent Witness*, is the only mainstream film I am aware of that assumes the female gaze and implicitly feminist stance of the TV movies we have just analyzed. Actually, it resembles these films in many ways not at all typical of Hollywood. For one thing, it is as subtle as a sledgehammer in its presentation of its message. For another, it is melodramatic in that lowest-common-denominator way associated with television. It is a down and dirty message film that pulls out all the corny stops in addressing and engaging its audience.

The thing that most struck me in watching *The Accused* and experiencing the sexually mixed audience response was that it could not possibly have been made—funded and promoted, as a major movie—if not for the influence, rarely commented upon but to me obvious, of the TV genre we are discussing. I have also had this thought about other recent films: *Stand and Deliver*, *Marie*, the biography of Ritchie Valens. All three are modeled on the formal and stylistic strategies of the TV movie. They are sentimentally melodramatic, narratively simple, and designed to manipulate audiences to sympathize with a hero or heroine in the most obvious ways.

The Accused, however, stands alone as a veritable feminist tract. Focusing on the victim, rather than inventing a female witness/heroine, it takes on all sorts of tricky issues. Sarah, the heroine, is the prototypical girl who "asked for it." She is a cocktail waitress who dresses suggestively, smokes dope, drinks, and runs her sex life according to her own rules. When she clearly comes on to a guy in the bar, even engaging in some pretty hot foreplay, and then breaks it off and starts to leave, three men rape her while most of the others cheer them on.

Unlike *Silent Witness*, *The Accused* has a second woman protagonist, an uptight yuppie lawyer who gradually comes to respect Sarah and the principles by which she lives. Sarah defies the double standard, stands up for herself against slights, and fights for her right to live as she sees fit without fear of male aggression. The film, predictably, sees her—and all these unconventional, socially threatening attitudes—vindicated. The differences from the TV movie are telling. There is no family here, for one thing. These two women are seen as independent operators, defined by their very different lifestyles, not their family situations. Sarah lives in a sleazy trailer camp; Kathleen, her attorney, lives in a high-rise condominium. Sarah wears tight jeans and sweaters; Kathleen wears discreet, dress-for-success suits.

The focus of *Accused* is sexual mores, of *Witness* family conventions. Still, they work in similar ways to hook the spectator into the heroine's point of view. For one thing, both use big stars and promises of sexual sensation to draw audiences. Without Jodie Foster and Kelly McGillis, *The Accused* might have gone the way of independent women's films like *Desert Hearts*, a film about lesbianism, which drew small box office receipts because of its "specialized" appeal.

Most importantly, though, both movies use the kind of melodramatic shtick associated with male stars like Sylvester Stallone and Clint Eastwood to rile up audiences. When I saw *The Accused* I was amazed to hear the males around me rooting for Sarah and booing the men in the bar. That is no small thing. It made me recall the first time I saw *Mildred Pierce*, as a very small child. This film, which I continue to see periodically, almost as a compulsion, gave me nightmares on and off for years. Without knowing why, I felt it held an ominous message for me, a child already dreaming of becoming a writer, a "career woman." Of course I understand now what I could not understand then: this film, like the goriest of woman-in-danger B movies today, presented a terrifying message to every woman who felt even marginally trapped and dreamed of escaping the prison of patriarchal roles and norms. It told us we might fly high for a while, might have success, accomplishment, even "unladylike" but thrilling sex. But eventually our pact with the devil would catch up with us. We would lose our human qualities, become vicious and cold, lose our husbands and children, and ultimately be brought very low indeed.

The Accused and *The Burning Bed* do not have the kind of nightmare power that comes from art that treats unresolvable contradictions in the context of a world that will not allow difference or change. They tie things up in a neat, oversimplified bow. They exaggerate the amount of change that is actually possible through sheer individual effort. Nonetheless, as women's drama, they deserve recognition for the positive and powerful message they provide the millions of women who see them.

4

TV Movies As Women's Genre

In the preceding chapter, I did two things. First, I placed the telefeature in the context of feminist film and media theory, since, as I hope is by now obvious, I believe the best of the form is more often than not found in movies that treat women's issues from the subject position of the female viewer, for reasons that grow out of the structure and dynamic of the industry itself. In this, I was being theoretically polemical. Feminist debates and theories about "women's culture" are very often on the cutting edge of critical discourse these days. But they have too often privileged certain kinds of popular culture over others because of clear theoretical biases about what stylistic and narrative strategies are most important or interesting. These biases have led to a near-total ignorance of TV movies because their formal properties do not fit the currently fashionable critical criteria.

My second goal in the previous chapter was to analyze in detail two works that I consider exemplary. In doing this, I was making a political value judgment: the most exciting and effective telefeatures are those that engage major social and political concerns from a feminist stance. *The Burning Bed* and *Silent Witness* both smack of propaganda—very effective propaganda, in my view—because they combine a strong ideological component with an equally strong appeal to emotion.

But this is only one part of the story of TV movies about women and women's issues. The other is the vast number of far less original or ideological films about women that make up the largest single "type" of the form. In this chapter I want to look at this class of telefeatures as a whole. I want to see what they have in common and how, as a class of TV programming, they form a subgenre that is enormously appealing to audiences—mostly female audiences—in spite of (or perhaps because of) their predictability and even (by the standards of "high art" criticism) mediocrity.

Alvin Marill's 1986 compendium of all the TV movies made up to that time verifies that women's films make up a clear majority. That fact in itself warrants particular attention to women's films. While the project of this study is the telefeature as a whole, there is no getting away from the fact that films dealing with women dominate and therefore deserve more thorough analysis than others.

My approach here will be largely based in genre theory. I have purposely chosen five films (I could have chosen fifty) that are typical, pedestrian, even clonelike. Most TV movies are. But I will argue that that very feature is a major clue to their vast popularity with women viewers. These films are almost ritualistic, and in my view that is not a bad thing. Needless to say, we are not talking aesthetics here, in the traditional critical sense. We are talking sociology as well as genre theory; we are dealing with the role of TV films in the lives and psyches of their fans. But we are not talking about simplistic, noncontradictory texts either. On the contrary, these texts exist as arenas of contested terrain, what political theorist Ernesto Laclau has called "ideological class struggle."

In this analysis, I am diverging from a particular kind of analysis that comes out of the British cultural studies movement, but that is now, as Meaghan Morris has aptly observed, something of a "boom industry" (Morris 1990). This movement, a reaction to the excesses of the Frankfurt School manipulation theory gang, has too often overstated, or misstated, the "liberatory" or "subversive" effects of popular culture. Where the Frankfurt crowd insisted that media were a monolithic, manipulative arm of the ruling class, this new school insists that the reader has enormous power over the text, that she or he can actually "negotiate" readings in ways that allow for totally new and subjective interpretations and meanings (see especially Fiske 1987, Radway 1984, and Ang 1985).

Somewhere between these two extremes there is a far more complicated reality. There is, after all, a dominant text or preferred reading. And readers have a limited ability to negotiate that text. We come to a text with different experiences, beliefs, and values—and even in different moods at different times. Neither of these truisms is entirely useful, however, in explaining the ideological and emotional workings of TV movies. It is more fruitful, I believe, to view such texts as inherently contradictory, posing certain dilemmas of female experience without resolving them ideologically, although they do resolve them emotionally. This approach eliminates the need to see TV programming as wholly repressive or wholly subversive. Instead, it allows us to focus on the *way* in which these texts present and resolve feminine dilemmas. Any number of works grapple with this complex issue in one way or another. In attempting to avoid a vulgar left reading, a critic like Julie D'Acci, for example, in her study of the "Cagney and Lacey" series, speaks of popular forms that "enable change and difference" and those that "limit them" (D'Acci 1987, 204). Tania Modleski, in *Loving with a Vengeance*, speaks of works that incorporate "moments of resistance" to dominant ideology even as they ultimately placate women caught in unpleasant and oppressive situations (Modleski 1982, 57). What such theories aim for is an understanding of how women use popular forms in ways that are healthy rather than debilitating.

This kind of approach I think is on the right track, no matter what the formulation, because it understands the contradictory nature of popular culture and neither condemns nor valorizes it. Janice Radway's work on romance novels is particularly instructive here. She found that the most popular romances centered on real fears experienced by women in today's sexual landscape and then put those fears to rest in ways that were clearly unrealistic but nonetheless soothing. (Radway 1984, 184 and 205). She sees these romances as serving a therapeutic function in the sense that they act as "a kind of cultural safety valve," and she analyzes them in terms of the role of myth in human experience: "They exist to relate a story already familiar to the people who choose to read them" (198). This is exactly how TV movies function for their viewers. They are predictable; they tackle scary matters of concern to women; and they invariably resolve the (essentially unresolvable) dilemma in ways that are cathartic and soothing by fudging ideological contradictions. I do not want to go too far with Radway, however. I am more concerned than she with ideological limits imposed on popular forms by the industry that produces them. Still, for the purposes of this discussion, her work is useful in explaining why lowest-common-denominator narratives are satisfying to so many viewers, repetitive and simplistic as they may be.

The Rules of the Game

Before getting into the texts themselves, we need to analyze the generic conventions of which they are constructed in a way that is different from our approach in chapter 3, where I made distinctions between films that pushed the limits of their generic conventions and those that did not. I am not interested in that issue here. I am interested, specifically, in the peculiar qualities that characterize telefeatures about women as women. What is a women's genre, after all? How have TV movies formulated the terms through which feminine identity is represented? That is the thrust of the chapter. But first I want to look once more, from a different angle, at the nature of generic forms themselves.

Let us start with Thomas Schatz's analysis of the workings of genre in the film industry. Schatz is interested in the way in which the Hollywood studio system developed a kind of formula for producing popular narrative that satisfied economic as well as emotional needs. The studios, interested in maximizing profits as efficiently as possible, understood that mass audiences existed in two separate ways. On the one hand, we come to popular culture as members of a shared society. On the other hand, we wish to be entertained, to be removed, temporarily, from the real world and its real problems. And then there are the very specific conditions under which films are produced. Filmmaking, especially in the Hollywood studio system, is a thoroughly collective process. It is not about *auteurs* with private, idiosyncratic artistic visions. In fact, it is one of Schatz's major—and most insightful—theses that the *auteur* theory of filmmaking is largely incorrect in its understanding of how Hollywood movies are made (Schatz 1981).

This point is also important ideologically. It flies in the face of what Schatz calls the "elitist critical assumption that art has an asocial, terminal value—that the artwork is an end in itself, somehow disengaged from the mundane trappings of its initial sociocultural environment" (14). He attributes this bias to the "academic or scholarly context in which we are generally exposed to the high arts . . . because we do study traditional artworks with little concern for the social imperatives involved in their creation . . . and presume that aesthetic objects do in fact 'transcend' the culture in which they were produced" (14).

Film critic Robin Wood echoes this thesis in an essay entitled "Ideology, Genre, Auteur" (Wood 1977, 284) in which he suggests that genre study is seriously weakened by its failure to place its analyses in a broad sociocultural context that includes the filmmaker(s), the production system, and the audience. Both these critics introduce a way of looking at genre narrative, often considered schlock, as something much more important and interesting. In fact, genre films (and TV movies are simply the logical extension of this form) are rather complex and contradictory forms.

On the one hand, to use Schatz's terms, they are static forms. They follow structural and thematic patterns that do not change. The crime film, for example, always pits a "good" cop against a "bad" criminal. It is always set in an urban environment and presents stereotypical representations of men and women. Westerns, domestic melodramas, romantic comedies, and other genres also are recognizable by certain standard components. As often as not, certain actors and actresses are typecast in stereotypical roles. Structurally, each genre type fulfills a certain kind of sociocultural fantasy. Something perceived as "natural" is disrupted: a gunslinger enters a peaceful western town; a romantically involved couple, or a family, are set at odds by some external event. In the end, harmony, justice, and peace are restored and the values upon which genre narrative rests are reinstated.

These values are also standard and predictable. In Westerns, social harmony, the sense of belonging to an intact community, is paramount. In domestic and romantic narrative, the sanctity of the family is implicitly valorized above all else. One need not think too long to see that these generic conventions are as valid today as they were in the thirties and forties. *Fatal Attraction*, *Pretty Woman*, and the many current crime films of the *48 Hours*/*Lethal Weapon* variety are genre films of the first order, no different in theme or structure from the films of Douglas Sirk, the endless list of romantic comedies in which the poor girl gets the rich guy, or the film noir offerings featuring Bogart and Cagney. The *Rocky* films, for that matter, are no different generically from the the old John Garfield-type films about immigrant youths rising to the top of the sports world.

But that is only half the story. The films just listed, and others, share many similarities but also differ from one another in many ways. To quote Schatz again, genre narrative is both static and dynamic (16). What is dynamic in genre film relates to cultural, social, and historic changes in the way we live, to what we, as a society, believe to be true or right, and to the way in which history has affected us. There is an innocence in the classic romantic and crime films that is clearly irrelevant to today's world. *When Harry Met Sally*, for example, is a romantic comedy about the mating game in the eighties. It is filled with all sorts of things that Fred Astaire and Ginger Rogers could not have dreamed of. Sexual mores are the most obvious example. But there are others. The world of singles today is informed by a host of issues Hollywood in the thirties did not need to consider. Marriage is no longer seen as the only inevitable conclusion to a relationship, nor as the only happy ending for women. The women in the old movies did have careers surprisingly often, but this was not foregrounded as an issue. And, while women in today's romances do invariably (and true to generic conventions that are static) end up married, the industry is not naive enough to present this in the same Jane Austenish we-must-get-Alice-married-off way.

In crime stories we see similar changes within the context of static conventions. Yes, there is a good cop who saves the day. But he is never (except in campy nostalgia films like *Dick Tracy*) free of the taint of at least some kind of vice of his own. No one plays by the rules any more because, true to the sense of our age that innocence is over, the industry knows that no one would buy it.

From Film Genre to TV Genre

In looking at the most conventional TV movies, I want to use this model of genre fiction as a set of conventions that are made up of a combination of static and dynamic elements. I think these two elements account for their popularity. They are at once reassuring and relevant, old-fashioned and up to date.

Another important aspect of the TV movie is similar to the films that came out of the old Hollywood studio system. In its prime the studio system operated as a kind of factory, an assembly line. Studios maintained crews and rosters of actors under contract to produce perhaps twenty films a year—a figure unheard of today when major stars may make as few as one or two films a year. Today's films are not connected to that socialized workplace of the past. Packagers put together deals based on a one-time collaboration of a group of independent artists—stars, directors, cinematographers, and so on.

TV networks, like the old studios, commit themselves to a season's worth of programs—including for television perhaps twenty telefeatures. Budgeting and time constraints necessitate assembly-line production systems. TV movies are made fast and with the constant involvement of network personnel. Networks have special departments that do nothing but work up these features from conception to final wrap. They tend to use the same writers and directors, and very often the same actors, for these films (see Gitlin 1984, 115–43). They also tend to use the same proven formulas, since ratings and profits matter above all. They play it safe. But they also pay close attention to what, by their lights, are the vicissitudes of the zeitgeist. The static/dynamic model describes this system perfectly.

We have already established that it is the woman's genre that dominates TV movies. Looking at this phenomenon, however, is tricky. On the one hand, we have a mind-boggling list of telefeatures about women that are sometimes indistinguishable one from another. On the other hand, however, we can separate out specific thematic emphases rather neatly. Even here, though, when we look very closely at these different "types" of movies, they tend to blur, to become far less distinct than their *TV Guide* blurbs or a casual viewing might indicate. There are intricate overlaps and combinations of various structural and thematic features in virtually all of these movies.

It is this generic blurring that I wish to analyze here, because it gives a clue to the appeal of the form and to the strategy of the networks. The dynamic aspects of the form are of course present, but they are not as dramatic as one might think. One reason for this is the very short history—a mere twenty years—of the form. Stylistic and cultural differences are fairly minimal. Still, they do exist, most notably in the changes wrought in cultural and political values during the Reagan/Bush years. Sexual freedom and the importance of careers and independence for women—so pronounced (at least for television) in the seventies—virtually disappeared in the eighties. In place of "doing your own thing," children have become all important. This is not to say that sexual liberation and feminine autonomy were ever, ultimately, valorized in TV movies. The importance of family values was, as we have seen, always primary for TV drama generally. But in the seventies the emphases were clearly different. No matter that everyone ended up in a family and ultimately lived for family values. Issues of sexual liberation and feminine autonomy were nonetheless taken seriously, even if the penalties for such behavior were severe in the end. Today, they are simply not hot topics, except in rare cases. Parenting, stepparenting, helping troubled children—these are the themes of the day.

The most dramatic conclusions one comes to by surveying the vast realm of women's features are that they tend to fall almost exclusively into a few categories and that each category tends to incorporate features from all the others. There is, then, a kind of master narrative at work in this genre and it is easy to define. In planning this chapter, I went through Marill's 1986 list of TV movies and tried to classify all the women's films according to a set of thematic categories that seemed to define the terrain. Domestic family issues, women overcoming illnesses, "star" biographies, sexual issues, issues involving children (not necessarily in families), women confronting social or political issues, and women in danger—whether from sexual or domestic violence or psychopathic stalkers—were the categories that virtually every telefeature fell into. Simple enough.

Looking more closely, however, it turned out not to be so simple at all. While two categories—family drama and sexual drama—clearly dominated the field, it was often difficult to be sure which category even these films belonged in. Moreover, examples of the other categories as often as not could be classified very differently. A movie about a social worker treating an abused child, for example, had many characteristics of family drama. A movie about a prostitute similarly tended to fit nicely into the family drama category since its narrative thrust, its resolution, invariably moved toward that institutional ideal.

In the end, I chose to analyze five films typical of a particular category, each of which, inevitably, has strong generic links to other categories. The choices were in some ways arbitrary. For each film, there were also many—often scores—of others that were similar and in some cases even identical. In looking at these films, I intend two things. First, I want to interrogate the appeal of the genre in terms of feminist and genre theory. And second, I want to lay out the parameters of the form—what is universal and ideologically coherent about all TV movies about women.

In every category of telefeatures dealing with specifically female issues there is a thematic and a structural constant. Thematically, there is the issue of defining the concept of "woman" in an age when female identity is most definitely in social flux and therefore a matter of contested terrain. The first thing we need to confront, then, is the strategy developed by the genre for negotiating this concept. In this regard the work of Teresa de Lauretis and Annette Kuhn is particularly useful. In de Lauretis's *Alice Doesn't: Feminism, Semiotics, and Cinema* there is a useful working definition: "By 'woman,' " she writes, "I mean a fictional construct, a distillate from diverse but congruent discourses in Western cultures. . . . By women, on the other hand, I mean the real historical beings who cannot as yet be defined outside of those discursive formations, but whose material existence is nonetheless certain" (1984, 5). Kuhn, in her *Power of the Image*, has addressed the same issue—the distinction between representational "woman" and historically and socially actual women. "Meanings," she writes, "do not reside in images. They are circulated between representation, spectator and social formation" (1985, 5).

In other words, the constructions of "woman" in media representations, and the meanings that accrue to such constructions, must be understood as negotiated meanings in which the spectator, the industry, and the larger social world in which real women act—as individuals and very often as political actors (the existence of the women's movement as a political force in all our lives and consciousnesses cannot be overestimated as a factor in media constructs)—all figure, often in contradictory ways. Add to that the importance of the role of feminists within the industry, the way in which the system of publicity influences spectator expectations and responses, and the role of ratings in determining how representations are constructed and you have a very complex process indeed.

At the conservative end of the spectrum we are analyzing, we have the already discussed need for the industry to reinforce the most traditional meanings of womanhood. Most TV movies (and other forms of TV narrative) lock women into a very traditional mold. No matter what happens in the movies, their ultimate message is still that women are predominantly—we may say essentially—represented as wives and mothers. Sexually unconventional women are invariably fated to either reform or to come to a bad end.

At the other extreme, however, we have radical interventions in many of these movies that are far more progressive, or perhaps I should say transgressive. Because of what producers and networks know about the power and popularity of feminist discourses, and because of the growing number of feminists involved in producing these texts, there are almost always elements in TV movies that speak to the changing roles of women in society with sympathy and support. Filmmaker Michelle Citron has written a fascinating essay on the positive aspects of women's increasing involvement in mainstream popular film and video production. As a filmmaker associated, for many years, with alternative feminist media, she has come to appreciate the possibilities and importance of working "within the context of old genres, while creating a different point of view or subverting it in some other way" (Czitrom 1988, 59). She uses as her prime example the work of Hollywood director Martha Coolidge and spends a good deal of time analyzing the film *Valley Girl* in an intriguing and audacious way. While most critics and filmmakers would surely consider this teen flick beneath contempt, Citron takes it very seriously indeed. She points out, of course, that certain aspects of the film—particularly the nudity and lowest-common-denominator generic conventions—were "demands made by the producer, not the director." Still, she argues, "Coolidge is able to work within the constraints of a popular genre and subvert it in small but significant ways by offering a point of view informed by a feminist consciousness" (61).

Lisa Lewis, in her groundbreaking study of women and rock music, *Gender Politics and MTV*, makes a similar case for the music videos of Cyndi Lauper, Madonna, Tina Turner, and Pat Benatar and analyzes Susan Seidelman's film *Desperately Seeking Susan*, which features Madonna playing a Madonna-like character (Lewis 1990). In both of these studies, the issue of female subject positions in popular forms and the role of the spectator/fan in actively creating or negotiating meanings figure prominently.

When we look at TV movies we find the same kind of contradictory strategies, although the form itself—geared to wives and mothers occupying domestic space rather than teenagers not yet settled into adult roles and at a stage of life where rebellion and exploration of options are central—is far more conservative and less daring. Still the concept of negotiation is key in these texts, and they are best approached in terms of negotiations and their always inconclusive resolutions.

Classic Texts

In each of the movies I will now analyze, the problematic of "womanhood" is central, as is the negotiation among the various forces named earlier in an attempt to represent the always uneasy and ideologically incoherent (to use Stuart Hall's words) construct of "woman" in the decades following the second wave of feminism. While the category of films about professional women whose work involves treating the problems of troubled children is among the smallest, I am going to begin with one such film, *A Child's Cry*, because it exemplifies the generic overlapping that is characteristic of all these films.

In this movie, made in 1986, an intensely dedicated social worker confronts a typical 1980s problem: the sexual abuse of a small child, in this case a boy. At the beginning of the narrative, Joanne is suffering burnout because she has, for many years, worked in an agency that deals with issues of domestic and sexual violence. She is presented as independent, implicitly as a feminist, and in general as a pretty tough cookie. When she loses her temper in a session with a grossly sexist wife batterer whose wife reneges on her decision to press charges, her supervisor transfers her to a child welfare agency. It is not insignificant that the narrative shifts from issues of sexual violence to child abuse. It is almost paradigmatic of the recently changing emphases of women's TV movies away from the sexual battlefield and toward concern for children.

The predictable plot is classic. At first Joanne suspects the boy's father, a single parent whose wife has left and allowed him custody because her high-powered career keeps her traveling a lot. Matt, the father, appears at first to be the worst kind of autocratic, nonnurturing type, given to temper tantrums and excessively private about his life and feelings.

As in the classic romance genre, the apparently cold, unapproachable, insensitive male gradually bends under the influence of Joanne's concern and affection for his son. In the end, the real culprit turns out to be the boy's Little League coach. There is a clear implication that Joanne and the father will ultimately get together to form a "real" family. Both are loners. Both have had extremely unsatisfactory family lives. Joanne herself was raised by her father because her mother died when she was an infant.

In the course of the narrative, Joanne confronts her father, who has always been distant and unavailable to her emotionally. Thus we have several layers of discourse, all of which are contradictory and ideologically incoherent. On the one hand, of course, Joanne is a thoroughly modern career woman, self-sufficient, assertive, committed to her work. But on the other hand, she is also a woman who is lonely and needs the kind of nurturance and support that come with a traditional family (as they are presented on television, of course).

The most emblematic scene in the film, and the one that spells out the contradictions most dramatically, is the one in which Joanne, Matt, and the child are foregrounded in an idyllic natural setting that reeks of traditional family ideology while in the background the villain stands menacingly overlooking the happy unit. There is no mistaking the message here. Sexual abuse of children is a threat to all we hold dear. Once the villain is purged, the three lonely principals are free to form an Edenic life together.

This movie is satisfying because it resolves the contradictions between feminism and traditional life. It allows the heroine to retain her New Woman characteristics and also achieve the traditional feminine role of wife and mother. Janice Radway, in her study of romances, makes the point that the most popular and successful works "deal convincingly with female fears and reservations by permitting them to surface briefly . . . and then explicitly laying them to rest" (158). The fear, in this case, is of loneliness and emotional emptiness, a very real fear for the "liberated woman." It is laid to rest by providing the heroine with a family. But she still has her career, her strength and independence, her dignity. This is the best of all possible worlds, the fantasy of "having it all." In real life, of course, it is not so easily achieved. Thus the satisfaction of such narratives.

This movie resembles a great many other telefeatures even though it is not as common a generic formula as others. In fact, I found only six other movies that fit the category of nonmothers devoted to helping troubled children. But here is where the generic overlaps come in. In the largest category of women's films, the family drama, the same issues come up over and over again. Films like *Another Woman's Child*, about the difficulties of becoming a stepmother, *Kids Don't Tell*, *Something about Amelia*, *Children of Divorce*, *Sarah T.*, and *Circle of Violence*, all about child abuse within the family, *Adam*, about a missing child, *The Child Stealer*, about a divorced father who kidnaps his child, *Angel Dusted*, about a teenager addicted to the drug PCP, *Last Cry for Help* and *Silence of the Heart*, both about teen suicide, are all—and they are merely a relatively small sample—about problems of children within the context of an actual family, intact or not. And there are of course myriad examples of films about women juggling careers while caring for children and husbands.

What these movies have in common, and what makes them so popular, is their common concern with irreconcilable contradictions faced by modern women. They all present their narratives from a female subject position and they all negotiate the meaning of "woman" in tricky ways. Women are always, ultimately, defined in terms of traditional roles. But the definitions always acknowledge the difficulties of those roles and treat them with seriousness and respect. There is always a subtext that challenges the dominant text and allows for divergent readings. To be sure, as Jameson has demonstrated, popular narratives always have an element of utopianism in their resolutions. But that is not all they have. The work of Michel de Certeau is particularly useful in analyzing these texts. In *The Practice of Everyday Life* (1984) he rightly makes a distinction between two elements of popular culture that are at odds. While acknowledging the element of utopianism in popular texts, he insists that such texts also include what he calls "polemological practices" and that there is always a movement between these two poles in popular culture. By polemological practices he means those elements of popular texts that articulate, to use Meaghan Morris's terminology, "loss, despair, disillusion, anger" (Morris 1990, 25). This sense of "failure" ensures that popular texts retain an element of political seriousness and relevance. It is also the reason that such texts—banal as they may be—are intellectually interesting.

In the case of *A Child's Cry*, for example, the pleasure comes from the utopian resolution. But the critical interest it holds rests on the contradictions it can never resolve. From the female spectator's perspective, Joanne is a complex and contradictory figure, after all. She is at once modern and even transgressive in her persona as an actor in the public sphere. But she is always a traditional woman as well. One way in which this contradiction is made manifest is her style of dress. Radway has pointed out that readers understand clothing codes as a kind of "shorthand" that reveals deeper aspects of character and ideological meaning. In *A Child's Cry*, Joanne dresses in a way that is understated and clearly not stereotypically feminine. She wears flat shoes, sensible skirts and sweaters, a functional hairdo. She is presented as neither a dress-for-success yuppie nor a frilly, girlish type. This is important in portraying her as down-to-earth, serious, and unpretentious. Similarly, her home is—especially by TV movie standards—unpretentious and underdecorated. Still she is attractive in conventional terms. She is definitely not asexual although this is played down in the text and is primarily understood through the visual cultural details.

As we examine the other movies on other subjects, these details will figure equally prominently. The producers walk a kind of tightrope in creating TV movies, and so do the networks. They know their target audience well, and they understand the need to address conflicting needs, interests, and desires. Finally, the viewer herself has conflicting attitudes and emotions that must be addressed in ways that allow for individual readings that are neither too conservative nor too daring. The success of women's telefeatures rests on all these considerations.

By far the largest category of women's telefeatures is the one that represents the heroine as first and foremost a wife and mother confronting family crises. The film I chose to analyze here is *An Early Frost*, made in 1986 and dealing, ostensibly, with a male protagonist—a young man with AIDS. As is so typical of TV movies, however, the implied address is to women—mothers—who make up the bulk of the audiences. Like the very similar pre-AIDS movie *Consenting Adults*, its real theme is less the drama of "coming out" for the young gay man than the trauma to his traditional family. This is equally true of the many films about juvenile crises—teen suicide, teen drug and alcohol addiction, teen prostitution, teen victimization by sexual abuse or adult violence, or the effects of divorce on children. In this sense it is no different from the myriad features about marital crises—adultery, divorce, women entering the workforce, conflicts over abortion, even aging and weight gain. All these works operate in the same generic way. A woman faces and overcomes a socially common problem and manages to bring her husband and/or children around to a healthy attitude and behavior. The audience identifies, primarily, with the woman who is—as in *A Child's Cry*—represented in terms of a contradictory but emotionally soothing combination of traditional and nontraditional traits.

In *An Early Frost* the establishing scenes are typical. A prosperous, suburban family, fully equipped with a large, rambling, lavishly furnished home—there is even a picket fence—is about to celebrate the mother's birthday with an elaborate dinner. The family consists of a businessman father, a mother who gives piano lessons at home, and a pregnant daughter and her husband and child. The missing member, a son who is a successful Manhattan lawyer they rarely see, suddenly shows up as a surprise. His life is seen, by the family, as secretive and aloof, but they never suspect the reason: he lives with another man and cannot bring himself to tell his family—especially his macho father.

As it turns out, the son has chosen to come out at last because he has AIDS. That the young man will die is a foregone conclusion and therefore not the dramatic fulcrum of the narrative. It is, rather, the mother, who typically confronts the crisis and brings healing not only to the father-son relationship but even to the rift between her son and his estranged lover, who has probably caused the disease by his occasional (never before admitted) sexual flings.

To understand the real message of the film—the importance of standing by family members and (in this case) long-term lovers, no matter what—it is useful to refer to the theories of Nancy Chodorow and other feminist object-relations theorists who have analyzed the differences in male and female character structures and relations to the world as a function of the effects of traditional mothering. Girls, they say, raised primarily by the same-sex parent, develop a sense of themselves as "self-in-relation" to others, with confused and permeable ego boundaries. Boys, on the other hand, raised by the opposite-sex parent, develop a need to separate and to see themselves more in relation to the external world as a way of separating from the mother (Chodorow 1978, 169–70).

Whether this theory holds true is not at issue here. (Personally, I find it less than compelling for a number of reasons. For one thing, I am not convinced by psychoanalytic interpretations, which deny the reality of enormous differences among women— particularly women of other than white middle-class cultures. They also ignore the issues of single-parent and homosexual families, which obviously do not fit the presumably universal paradigm implied in such thinking.) TV movies, like Chodorow's theories, for the most part assume heterosexual, middle-class, traditional family structures, and therefore her ideas fit nicely with their ideological and emotional strategies.

In the case of *An Early Frost* this is a particularly useful vantage point because the father is Chodorow's classic nonnurturant, world-involved figure, while the mother and the daughter are wholly relational in their behaviors and positions in the world. What is most intriguing about this film is the way in which the son, Michael, is presented. On the surface, he is traditionally masculine. He is played by Aidan Quinn, an actor who is totally devoid of any effeminate mannerisms. Michael's work is worldly and all-consuming; it exists in the realm of power and wheeling and dealing. Still, when his homosexuality becomes his defining characteristic, which, as the disease progresses, it must, he takes on more traditionally feminine traits. He is vulnerable, needy, unable to maintain his aloof self-sufficiency. This is emphasized in a somewhat digressive subplot involving his split with his lover, Peter. It would seem, on the surface, that Michael's anger was more than justified. He has been monogamous; Peter has cheated and in the process given Michael a death sentence. But in their final argument another issue is raised and presented as valid. Peter, whose own family has known of his lifestyle and met and embraced Michael, is enraged that Michael has kept their relationship secret not only from his family but from his business associates. This, he argues, is a kind of rejection that justified his feeling less than committed to the monogamous relationship.

So how does the mother deal with all of this?—for that is our main concern here. The contrast between the two parents is extreme. At the birthday dinner the father jokes about the typical parental concern: when are you going to bring a girl home for us to meet? Later, when Michael says "I'm gay; I have AIDS," his father actually strikes him. Still later, when the father—who refuses to speak to his son for the duration of the visit—is faced with an emergency that involves dealing with the outside institutional world, he has a dramatic change of heart. The incident is played for all the high drama possible. Michael goes into convulsions, and the ambulance drivers, when they realize he has AIDS, refuse to take him to the hospital. Again the father resorts to violence, this time against the drivers. Certainly it is a change for the better. Still, the terms of the transformation are classically masculine. He acts out his rage against an institutional "policy" that he, as a man used to dealing with and even controlling external life, finds enraging.

It is the mother who, wholly unlike her spouse, is always caring and supportive, and she is the agent of reconciliation. In scene after scene, she confronts those who have problems accepting the truth. When she asks her husband to read an article about homosexuality and he insists that "I don't want to know," she insists, even more firmly, "You have to know." When her daughter, who has known about and accepted Michael's gayness, refuses to visit him because she is pregnant, the mother berates her as well. When the attending physician brushes off her demands for information, she holds her ground, more than assertively, until he finally takes the time to give her the information she needs to cope with the reality of the situation. And finally, when Peter, the estranged lover, calls, it is the mother who convinces Michael that he should reconcile with him because Peter clearly cares for him.

Throughout, she is portrayed as understandably shocked, troubled, and uncomfortable but nonetheless determined to break through everyone's reserve and alienation and bring love and understanding to the family. She interrogates Michael about his life with Peter. She consistently affirms the noncontingency of maternal love. She is a pillar of strength, sense, and compassion.

Again, we have an interesting negotiation of the meaning of womanhood. More than any of the other movies we will look at in this chapter, this heroine is a traditional mother with no career, no causes, no sexual or social issues complicating her life. The disease, after all, is not hers but Michael's. Still, the movie is an object lesson in how to be both a "good" mother and an independent, active agent in the world. While this movie has rightly received some acclaim for treating a controversial issue openly and honestly (unlike most TV treatments of AIDS, the victim is neither a child nor a woman but a gay male), it is nonetheless not so much about coping with the disease from the victim's point of view as from the mother's. What would you do, it asks in classic TV movie fashion, if you discovered your son was gay and/or had AIDS? It answers the question, again in classic style, with a moralistic object lesson in how to be a good mother. Its address, its subject position, is female and maternal. And like its many generic cousins, it is at once prescriptive and respectful of its heroine, a woman in a family but one who transcends the male-oriented representations of women as passive appendages and helpmates to the head of the house.

Sex and the Telefeature Heroine

Moving from family life to the experiences of women outside families, or at least transgressive of traditional family values, we see a different pattern. Sex sells, of course, and it is no surprise that the second-largest category of TV movies addresses sexually unconventional women. The film I am going to analyze is *Sharon: Portrait of a Mistress*, but I could have chosen one of dozens of similar narratives. We have already looked, in a different context, at *My Mother's Secret Life*, which negotiates our culture's endemic contradictions between sexual freedom and motherhood. And there are scores of others. In fact, the "Portrait" movies, most of which have been produced by Frank Von Zerneck, are a subgenre unto themselves. *Portrait of a Stripper, Portrait of a Showgirl, Portrait of a Teenage Runaway*, and *Portrait of a Centerfold* are only a few of the very popular movies about the lives of women who have crossed the line of bourgeois respectability but nonetheless are presented as conventional in their love for their children, their implied or explicit longing for a more conventional female life, and their struggles—sometimes successful, sometimes not—to escape their lifestyles. *Children of the Night, American Geisha*, and *Beverly Hills Madame* are a few more movies on the same theme.

Sharon happens to have an unhappy ending—she never gets "cured" and the final scene shows her continuing her old, bad ways, apparently for the rest of her sexually active life. But a close reading of the text reveals a moral identical to the movies in which the heroine does escape to conventional happiness. In other words, there are permutations on this theme but it is not necessarily the narrative closure that tells the tale. Rather, the subtext is the source of the "lesson" sent out to women viewers about the wages of sexual transgression.

That subtext is invariably couched in Freudian ideology. *Sharon* is the story of a successful businesswoman addictively drawn to older men, father figures who are married and therefore unavailable. We see her in the early scenes being rejected by her current lover, an older, married man for whom the affair was always just that—a temporary fling. Almost immediately, she finds a replacement, another father figure prone to intermittent sexual adventures but ultimately committed to his conventional wife and family.

The discourse in terms of which this drama is presented is overbearingly Freudian. Sharon's father died when she was young and she has spent her life, as the heavy-handed text makes endlessly clear, trying to find a replacement for the man whose death she has experienced as abandonment. The neatly organized narrative strategy is—as in all telefeatures—a series of ideologically loaded scenes in which those who care for her try to get her to recognize this pattern and seek help through psychotherapy. Three consecutive scenes bludgeon us with the idea that Sharon is on a self-destructive course and needs to recognize her impending (tragic) fate and change her behavior. First there is the ubiquitous best friend, happily married and devoted to her husband and kids, who consistently lectures her on her need to "see a shrink." In this scene the dice are loaded against Sharon. The friend tells her she is seriously worried about Sharon's future because her lifestyle is so self-destructive. Sharon responds with a comparison: "Every time you cop out and don't take your painting seriously" but choose instead "to have yet another baby," Sharon tells her friend, "I don't tell you to see a shrink." "That's different" says the happy homemaker. But is it really? Only in the context of the movie's Freudian discourse, which privileges traditional female roles over less conventional possibilities.

In the next scene, Sharon's assistant tells her that "My mother saw you having lunch with your father last week." The assistant knows, of course, that Sharon's father is dead. She is intentionally, if indirectly, letting Sharon know what her situation looks like to the outside world and how unhealthy it is. And then there is a scene in which Sharon's mother meets her lover—a business associate—and asks if he is available. "Dad's been dead twenty years," she tells her daughter, "and it's time I started looking around."

As the narrative moves to closure, the friend becomes increasingly insistent that Sharon "get some help." In a dramatic interchange, Sharon yells "Stop it! Stop it! Stop it!" and her friend yells back, "I can't, Sharon, I love you!" What these scenes add up to is the strong message that Sharon's sexual behavior is a sign of serious illness. Add to this a really nice guy who wants a real relationship and is fiercely rejected by Sharon because she is not able to function in a normal relationship with an appropriate, available man, and you have a morality tale as puritanical as any medieval text.

When her lover breaks with her in a particularly ugly scene in which he expresses amazement that Sharon did not understand the inevitability of the break, she hits bottom and does begin to see a psychiatrist. The ending, however, is as downbeat as the genre gets. Sharon moves from the West to the East Coast to start a new life. In the final scene, however, just before the credits roll, she attends a posh Manhattan party where she zeroes in on the one man who clearly fits her unhealthy pattern: an older, not particularly attractive but still successful-looking gentleman who is sitting by himself, oblivious to his surroundings. She catches his eye and the chemistry is immediately evident.

While most of the "bad girl" movies on TV end happily, with the stripper/centerfold/prostitute heroine finding a good man to love and save her, this one rejects the usual scenario. The young, attractive man she meets at a "How to Start Dating Again" seminar that her friend virtually drags her to, fails to interest her. He is, as she tells him, "a really nice guy," but she is just not his type.

Still, the appeal of this film, like the ones that manage to rescue their heroines from self-destruction in a variety of uplifting ways, is typical. For one thing, there is all that glamour and style. As is typical of TV movies made in the mid- to late seventies, clothing and sets—household decor, restaurants, department stores, and weekend getaways—are designed to make the mouths of average viewers, living in less tony environments, water. Sharon shops on Rodeo Drive and lunches elegantly. Even her most painful scene, the one in which her lover tells her their affair is over, takes place in a bathroom so luxurious it might have been designed by Danielle Steel or Judith Krantz. There she is, up to her neck in lush bubbles, sipping champagne from a crystal flute, hair beautifully and sexily pinned up, makeup intact.

There is such a complicated mixture of messages in this film that it is impossible to read it only as a simple morality tale. The mise-en-scène speaks its own language, and it is a language of desire—for glamour, sexual excitement, escape from the ordinary. Yes, we know that Sharon will end badly, even pathetically.

Yes, we know that a simpler, more conventional female life course would be more satisfying. Yes, we know that she is damaged emotionally in very serious ways. But for the moment, actually for the two hours that we live in Sharon's shoes, we cannot help but feel more than a little envious. She is independent, adventurous, and gorgeous. Avis Lewallen, in an analysis of the pulp novel and TV miniseries *Lace*, explains the contradictions and their appeal. She contrasts this genre, which she describes as "shop and fuck," with the more "serious" work of explicitly feminist writers and producers and makes a claim for their own kind of feminist implications (Lewallen 1989, 89).

Feminists, Lewallen argues, have made heterosexual sex itself a problematic issue, filled with "the contradictions involved in sexuality and representation." Lacanian theories about representation have insisted that women can occupy only "the object/other" position in conventional genres and therefore, for feminists, only "alternative representational structures" (100–101), structures of discourse that challenge convention, should be presented. Lewallen disagrees and so do I. There is, after all, a contradictory but very real pleasure in representations of women who experience the "excitement" of unconventional sexual behavior of the kind associated with prefeminist lifestyles and attitudes. That pleasure is complicated and made interesting by the counterplay, within the text, of other messages. The wages of sin are never forgotten; the woman's true salvation can come only when she gives up her old habits (and pleasures). Still, in acting out old-fashioned sexual rebelliousness, in refusing to be a good girl, the heroine is also, in a real sense, being very much her own woman, very much the transgressor of bourgeois convention.

In the more common form of this film, in which the woman does escape to conventionality, her life is generally not seen as quite so appealing. Even the mother in *My Mother's Secret Life* is presented as lacking in real pleasure, real intimacy of any kind. And the majority of these films feature women whose lives are downright oppressive. The many showgirls, strippers, hookers, and runaways on TV movies are struggling, running from really horrible family situations, raising children alone and on a shoestring, or in an emotional deep freeze that is clearly painful. These women are survivors, doing the only thing they can think of to get through. When a nice man comes to the rescue they are obviously relieved and grateful. In any event, what these movies and the ones about women like Sharon who do not escape, have in common is an absolute assumption that love, marriage, and motherhood is the best possible life for women. No matter that there are subtexts and contradictions. That, after all, is the condition of women today. We have choices and alternatives, many of them exceedingly attractive and even rewarding. And these two constructs of womanhood are always at war in narratives of transgression. No matter whether the conventional, "utopian" ending is enforced or not. There is a tug of war about the definition of modern womanhood that reflects but never wholly resolves this ideological tension. Bad girls are not "bad" in the traditional sense any more, even on television. They are a host of other more admirable things, ranging from strong and independent to glamorous and adventurous, girls who, in pop singer Cyndi Lauper's historically significant words "wanna have fun" and really do.

The Really Bad News:
When Transgression Leads to Death

One fascinating subgenre of women's TV movies is hard to categorize because the main character is sometimes a man rather than a woman. This is the set of films in which women are "in danger," are physically violated, murdered, or led to fatal self-destruction by some aspect of their characters or environments. There have been dozens of TV movies about rape victims, victims of domestic violence, and victims of psychopathic murderers. There are also a number of movies about stars, extraordinarily successful women who, at the prime of their success, are either killed or succumb to alcoholism, drug addiction, or—most recently—anorexia. *The Karen Carpenter Story*, in which a young woman rises to fame and is destroyed by anorexia, is typical. In this highly rated feature, the star system itself, and the tyranny of media images of beauty, are presented as the villains. In the films about sexual or domestic violence—*The Burning Bed*, *A Case of Rape*, and *Shattered Dreams* are just a few— patriarchal values and institutions cause the heroine's downfall.

And in films about psychopathic killers—husbands, more often than not—what Tania Modleski has called "the mystery of masculine motives" (Modleski 1982, 37) is to blame.

The appeal of such narratives is the same as the appeal, so aptly analyzed by Modleski, Joanna Russ, and others, of the Gothic romance. Russ has said that "gothics are written for women who are afraid of their husbands" (Russ 1973, 670). A lot of women are and should be. Stories of successful, apparently stable men who systematically attempt to kill, and sometimes succeed in killing, their wives are common in the headlines. It is a fact of life in sexist society. It is also no accident that these kinds of tales are almost invariably made into TV movies and miniseries. Women tend to be intrigued by the dynamics of a relationship that—while extreme—is psychologically familiar. The *"Women Who Love Too Much/Love Addiction"* phenomenon bears this out.

One telefeature that combines all these elements—the star bio, the woman-in-danger theme, and the profile of a psychopathic lover (a man who loves too much?)—is *Death of a Centerfold: The Dorothy Stratten Story*. This movie is particularly interesting to analyze because it has a theatrical film counterpart, *Star 80*, that is constructed very differently from the TV version. The differences are emblematic of the way in which TV movies tend to address female viewers and theatricals do not.

Dorothy Stratten was the small-town girl who, manipulated by her sleazy boyfriend, went to Hollywood, became a *Playboy* centerfold and the lover of both Hugh Hefner and Peter Bogdanovich, and—before the boyfriend murdered her—was being groomed for movie stardom by Bogdanovich, a respected director. The story is classic. The boyfriend, Snider, is a loser, a hustler always looking for the main chance. He meets Stratten when she is a teenager working as a waitress in a diner. He fills her head with grand schemes, takes her to the coast, and pushes her to sell herself to Hefner with him as her manager. As things progress, she outgrows him, and he is increasingly frantic over the prospect of losing her, the only good thing he has ever had in his life. As she becomes stronger and more independent, he becomes more and more crazed. Finally, he shoots her to death, just when she has moved in with Bogdanovich and is preparing to star in one of his films.

In the TV version, this is a tragic morality tale whose point is that a woman has the right to be confident and independent and need not be dependent on a man to create a life for her. We see her at first as a passive girl, lacking in self-esteem. Enter Snider, an older man who is overbearing, bossy, and domineering. Key scenes show him meeting her mother and sister, who both dislike him intensely, ordering her to change her clothes and makeup, and filling her head with schemes for fame and fortune that revolve around his power to control her.

As is typical of TV movies, there is a lot of footage of Stratten's home and family, her worried relatives, Snider's obnoxious behavior. In fact, Snider is portrayed one dimensionally, as offensive and a loser. Only Stratten, in her innocence, fails to see it. When she rises to the height of glamour and success, it is in the context of her own personal growth and talent. When she moves into the director's home, for example, it is, at first, a platonic relationship. She needs to escape Snider, and Bogdanovich wants to help because he respects and cares for her and believes in her talent.

In the final scenes, the importance of women friends is made much of. One friend tells her that she need not rely on Snider or any man because "You've got somebody. You've got Dorothy and you don't need a David or a Paul [Snider] or anyone else." Her hairdresser, in the scene just preceding her murder, tells her how proud she should be of herself and her accomplishments. "You've got it made, girl," she says admiringly.

And then the tragedy. She agrees, out of pity, to see Snider and he, in a jealous rage, brutally murders her. Like *The Karen Carpenter Story*, this movie ends with an implied utopian moment that is narratively overturned because of a past that, tragically, has caught up with her. Her previous passivity and lack of esteem, leading to her liaison with a psychopath, cannot be avoided. Those are the facts. Still, the overall picture of Stratten is of a young woman coming into her own, on the basis of her own merits.

The theatrical film could not be more different. For one thing, it focuses almost all its attention on the figure of Snider, who is presented as weak and pathetic, a figure deserving of pity. The film is constructed with far more complexity. "Witnesses" give testimony, much of it contradictory, about Snider's character. Great patches of the film are devoted to his idiosyncrasies, his emotional failings, his pathos. There is no doubt that this film is presented from the male point of view. Stratten is his crutch, and when she begins to outgrow him and develop her own strength, he literally falls apart. Where the TV character was a one-dimensional bully, the film character is a baby—weak, incompetent, and the object of no small amount of sympathy. The man is quite simply fascinating as a character who fits Nancy Chodorow's theories of male fear, helplessness, and ultimate rage at dependence on a strong woman. He never outgrows it and therefore he is doomed.

The contrast between these two versions of the same "true" story is dramatic. In one, the TV version, we have a woman's tale of escape from patriarchal constraints. In the other, the film version, we have a text that can be read as a backlash against feminism. A man is psychologically castrated by an increasingly powerful woman and is therefore, in a strange way, presented as a victim himself. The woman is a mere symbol.

In all the woman-in-danger TV films there is a similar pattern. The man is hateful. The woman, as she begins to resist his oppressive controlling behavior and his endlessly diminishing her as a person, is treated with more and more hostility. Physical violence escalates or else the man begins to plot the woman's death. In the end the woman generally escapes and the man is punished. Invariably, the situation is presented as determined by social conditions and/or male character failure (the two obviously are seen as connected).

So what is the pleasure in these narratives? Female triumph over male structures of feeling and behavior, clearly. Again, the contradictory nature of the narrative works to gratify a number of desires in the woman viewer. There is, first, the acknowledgment that it is the contradictory conditions of a woman's existence (see Modleski 1982, 82) that are the cause of her problems and not her inherently "feminine" nature. Even in *Sharon* the desire for adventure, glamour, and sexual ecstasy plays against the obvious Freudian message about female neurosis. In the other examples, we tend more often to see women as victims who triumph over their conditions. When they do not—when they end up dead, for example—they are still perceived as having triumphed, although it is a Pyrrhic victory.

Women As Rebels

A final category of TV movies about women that, although it is not very frequent, nonetheless deserves attention is the genre of films about women who actually take on social or political causes. The networks tend not to produce these kinds of dramas too often because they do not fit easily into the formula of family and sexuality as the prime arenas of women's activity. When they are done, they are invariably manipulated in ways that include traditional family values in their representations of the women rebels. *Fun and Games, A Matter of Sex,* and *The $5.20 an Hour Dream* all deal with work issues: women workers fight for equal rights, comparable worth, a way to break into the old-boy network.

Less common are the truly political dramas about women who devote their lives to righting social and political injustice. *Katherine: Portrait of a Revolutionary* is the fictionalized story of Diana Oughton, the wealthy young woman who became a revolutionary activist in the Weather Underground of the 1960s. It was remarkable enough in its sympathy for ultraleft politics to be an anomaly. More typical was *Choices of the Heart,* which told the story of Jean Donovan, a Catholic lay worker slaughtered with three nuns by right-wing Salvadoran troops while she was working for human rights in Central America. Both these films were extraordinary in their political perspectives. But both also emphasized, as is absolutely necessary in this genre, the importance of certain kinds of traditional feminine virtues: caring for others, devoting oneself to children and the elderly, and so on.

Lois Gibbs and the Love Canal, made in 1982, is a particularly interesting example of this genre. Lois Gibbs was a housewife living in an area in which the government had been dumping toxic waste, contaminating the environment and causing children to sicken and die of a variety of diseases. As in all these political films—and here is where they differ dramatically from the norm—the heroine ends up without a man. Gibbs (whose husband works for the plant causing the problem) not only develops from a passive, insecure homebody into a brilliant organizer, speaker, and leader, she also divorces her husband.

It is instructive to compare this film with *Silkwood*, a theatrical film about a similar issue. The terms of the narrative, the way in which atmosphere, character, and ultimate resolution work in these films could not be more different. Gibbs is presented, from start to finish, as a woman whose primary identity is that of a mother. Family is all in this film. From the establishing shots, during the credits—in which we see Gibbs pick up her husband at work, drive to a grade school performance in which their small child is featured, and then have dinner at a fast-food restaurant— the family angle is central. What causes the divorce is the very different definitions of family responsibility held by the two parents. For Gibbs the welfare of her children, physically and emotionally, is paramount. For her husband, it is the responsibility for financial support, for paying the bills, which is what his job at the plant allows him to do.

The narrative proceeds most conventionally. Gibbs becomes concerned that toxic waste may be the cause of her small son's endless, increasingly severe, bouts of illness. At first she is reluctant to act. She is terrified of speaking in public, of being unable to understand the technical data she needs to absorb in order to understand the situation.

Scene by scene, she gains confidence, enjoying her newfound sense of a calling. She goes door to door with a petition and finds that she has made friends with neighbors she has never even spoken to before. In this sense the film is an enactment of what the early women's movement was about: a group of working-class housewives joining together to confront the male power establishment. Gradually, Gibbs becomes a real leader, and she loves her new role and the feeling of being really good at something in the public sphere.

At first her husband is supportive. He coaches her on her early, quavering public speeches. But eventually, when her ardor becomes so intense, her commitment to leave their home and community intractable, he balks. He wants to return to their contaminated house. He does not want to leave his job. In the end they part, and Gibbs becomes a full-time public figure (as, in real life, she is today). But she never stops being a mother. Motherhood is in fact the basis of everything she does. That never changes. Activism and motherhood are seen as complementary in this narrative. She must become a public figure because she cares about her family. Again, there is the happy reconciliation of contradictory female qualities. Independence, public life, aggressiveness, even in a male world, go hand in hand with maternal concern and nurturing. Gibbs never stops being the sweet, somewhat insecure woman she once was. She simply forces herself to overcome her fears for her children's sake.

Comparing this movie with *Silkwood*, another based on a true story about a wife and mother turned activist, one sees immediately the very different parameters required by TV and Hollywood cinema. Karen Silkwood is a born rebel, a hard-drinking, dope smoking, sexually unconventional woman who has left her husband and children because she is almost compulsively individualistic and rebellious.

Silkwood is not an entirely likable character. She is abrasive, foul-mouthed, at times almost recklessly self destructive. As her obsession—for it is that—with uncovering the unsafe working conditions at the Kerr-McGee plant grows, even her lover and her best friend retreat from her. There is something totally "unconnected," to use an object relations term, about Silkwood. She seems incapable of finding a way to be in the world, in relationships, and is quite clearly and tragically destined for ultimate isolation and worse.

Where Lois Gibbs's relationship to family and community grows with her activism, Karen Silkwood is treated to a far darker destiny. She is persecuted, subjected to lethal doses of radiation, and finally—it is implied—driven off the road to her death by the agents of the company she has opted to take on single-handedly. She is a loner and ultimately a loser. The dark atmosphere of the film, its fascination with the tragic consequences of unconventional lifestyles and antisocial behavior, are chilling. One does not leave this film feeling that a good fight is even possible, no matter what the outrages of the opposition. There is a meanness about this film that would never appear in a TV movie. Silkwood has made certain choices and they have led, inevitably, to her isolation and death.

Silkwood does not play on contradictions in the definition of femininity as do TV movies. Rather, it is a cynical, dark film with an object lesson that must surely chill the heart of any female viewer who sympathizes with Silkwood's rebellious sense of outrage at conventional society and its rulers. *Lois Gibbs*, like all TV movies about women, is itself conventional, warm, and almost gooey in its affection for its good-hearted heroine. Family values and feminist values interact here in ways that allow both to be valued. That *Silkwood*, from an aesthetic perspective, is more interesting and sophisticated is obvious. Nonetheless, from a feminist perspective, Lois Gibbs, with all its inevitable contradictions, is clearly more positive in its view of women's ability to buck the system and win.

5
TV Movies As History:
Class, Race, and the Past

While TV movies have been rooted predominantly in the domestic sphere and, in particular, in women's experiences and issues, there are obviously many other matters that come up again and again in the genre and that need to be addressed. In particular, TV movies—mostly in the form of miniseries—have become, in sometimes alarming ways, the predominant discourse through which Americans, especially young Americans, are now "educated" about our national history. Series like *Winds of War* and *The Blue and the Gray* present dramatizations of major periods in our history—World War II and the Civil War, respectively—that are marked by a confusing jumble of actual events and fictionalized action. "Study guides" are sent out to high school and college teachers across the nation, many of whom then require students to watch the series as class assignments. Teachers are overworked and welcome relief from lesson plans and other class preparations. And in an age when most American kids have trouble with, and vocally resist, more traditional reading assignments, television is often seen as a necessary evil, the only form of historic discourse students are used to and like to watch.

Still, the use of TV movies as historic documents is more than problematic. Even without the issue of using them as educational tools there is the question—raised again and again in media theory debates—of the political implications of presenting even "progressive" messages in a form that many argue is inherently reactionary by its very aesthetic nature. Debates over realism and naturalism, which mainstream television adopts religiously as nar-

118

rative and stylistic givens, have been heated. They strike at the heart of the issues I am addressing in this study: is it possible to intervene in positive ways in the development of national consciousness while working in a commercial, politically conservative industry and using the dramatic techniques of Hollywood narrative?

A tangential but related issue, debated more among film and video makers than among media critics, is the issue of "alternative" video works that strive to deconstruct and broaden the political focus of mainstream media. This debate comes up mostly in discussions of independent works, done on relatively small budgets and limited to relatively small audiences, that artistically and politically could not be done on television.

In this context I wish to discuss a few key examples of telefeatures treating matters of history as well as race and class representaion. The debates about realism, and about the high/low, alternative/mainstream media clashes are important ones for our purposes. They raise issues that do not come up often, or in the same way, in feminist film and media debates. But there is no way to thoroughly address the impact of TV movies without spending some time getting into these debates and looking at movies that enter the public sphere as representations of race, class, and history.

I would like, first, to summarize briefly the terms of the debates and the positions of the most prominent participants. Then we will look at an "alternative" video documentary, *Who Killed Vincent Chin?* by Christine Choy and Renee Tajima, about matters of race, class, and economics in America. This is a documentary, and its terms of address and the breadth of its analysis of a complex event are very different from the TV movies about similar subjects. Nonetheless, the issues of realism, of the ability of alternative texts to "produce" radical, or at least unsettling, mind sets in viewers and thus—the implication is—to lead viewers to at least some kind of consideration of the importance and possibility of social change come up in studying this videotape in ways that are in my view problematic.

Having looked at this model, we will then look closely at three telefeatures, *Roots*, *Crisis at Central High*, and *The Executioner's Song*. The first two treat race issues in terms of specific, dramatic, historic events. *Roots*, of course, is a very long miniseries that overridingly stresses historic movements and processes. *Central High*, by contrast, is a conventional TV movie that presents a single event—the integration of the public schools of Little Rock, Arkansas, in the 1950s—through the eyes of a traditional TV movie heroine, a white, middle-class teacher concerned with the emotional impact of the event on herself and the students.

Race is actually a subject that comes up often on telefeatures and in all other forms of commercial television. It has been "named" and identified as a hot issue and an important one. This is absolutely not the case with matters of class. First of all, Americans do not think in terms of class. The term *blue collar* is the standard euphemism of our public discourse. For this reason, movies dealing with working-class characters, which, we will see, are very different from those about families or race, are never flagged in the publicity machinery as in any way addressing this political issue. Rather, in subtle ways, working-class people and their histories and characters are represented as "troubled" and worse, for reasons bearing no connection to economic status. *The Executioner's Song* is a moving narrative based on Norman Mailer's book about the life and destiny of Gary Gilmore, who achieved his fifteen minutes of celebrity when he demanded to be executed for the murder he committed and refused to allow his attorneys to appeal his sentence. Unlike the two racial films, however, there is no ideological message foregrounded as the obvious "theme." There is a rather subtle and intriguing clash of ideological perspectives on crime and criminals, but you have to dig (and be very conscious of what you are digging for) to ferret it out. Mostly, the film comes across as—and was certainly promoted as—a sensational story of pathological crime, violence, and retribution.

All three of these films, and the documentary we will look at first, are powerful, effective, and commendable in many ways. These are not the generic formula pieces we examined in the previous chapter. This is important because the debate about realism and alternative art demands to be tested with works that stand out as somehow exemplary. If there is a case to be made for the legitimacy of these works, and, more to the point, their potentially powerful effect on audiences, it will best be made (or discovered) in analyzing television's most serious efforts.

The Problematics of Realism and Popular Drama

The long-standing debate about the political implications of traditional realistic/naturalistic drama has been carried on primarily
among British critics, and it has focused on examples of a certain
kind of television drama that is quite foreign to American network
television. The political terms of critical debate, as well as TV narrative, in Britain are far more openly leftist in their assumptions
about what television can and should be doing than is ever possible in this country. As is clear from earlier chapters, the limits of
what can be done, even in the most admirable of cases, in commercial television in the United States are severe. Still, the British
debate is important here because—adjusting for the realities of
American political discourse as well as TV drama—it raises questions we must address in order to make any sort of case for the
at least partially progressive elements in American TV movies
about traditionally "political" subjects (as opposed to those
whose politics are primarily feminist, if anything, and therefore
not necessarily seen as really political by a male-dominated public
sphere).

The most trenchant engagement in these issues is found in the
extensive debate surrounding a 1975 historical drama series,
Days of Hope, which presents the experiences of an English
working-class family during the period from the imposition of
conscription in 1916 to the General Strike of 1926. The producers
had an unambiguously progressive agenda. According to one of
them, Ken Loach, "We want anyone who feels themselves to be
suffering from crises today, caught by price rises, inflation and
wage restraint, to watch the films and realise that all this has happened before. We hope they will learn from the opportunities
that were lost in 1926 and the defeats inflicted on the working
class at that time. We haven't given any solutions, though the
judgment we make is clear, I think, and stated for the record"
(Bennett et al. 1981, 302).

Clearly, this is engaged political television of a kind that we do
not see in the United States. No TV movie producer can approach
a network and pitch an idea couched so blatantly in political,
much less class, terms. When the series ran in Britain, it caused a
critical uproar in which writers, most notably Colin MacCabe,

121

identified with the *Screen* magazine perspective. MacCabe argued fiercely for its inherently reactionary nature, which he saw as a function of adopting a traditional realist form of presentation. The debate, reprinted in the British Film Institute publication *Popular Television and Film* (Bennett et al. 1981), went on for a good five years, years in which participants rethought their positions, and other theorists, including Raymond Williams, entered the debate.

MacCabe's position—and this is also the position of many radical critics—was quite simply that realism inevitably must end by leaving viewers satisfied with the status quo because the form itself works to create that mind set. It does this by "naturalizing" the workings of history in its presentation of events as "transparent." In other words, realism, a bourgeois form that is widely accepted as presenting reality in an unmediated way, does not challenge the terms of bourgeois society but accepts them as given and sees political struggle as merely a part of that larger reality. Thus it is impossible for viewers to see the underpinnings of how society works, to question its naturalness and its implicit unchangeability. Even when the script presents contradictions that challenge bourgeois hegemony, they are inevitably resolved in the terms of the dominant discourse that realism, as a form, cannot escape (MacCabe 1986, 310–19).

MacCabe calls for a radical form of dramatic narrative that, he insists, must be nonrealist, must call attention to the televisual apparatus at work in creating realist narrative and thus leave viewers questioning the validity not only of political institutions but also of the way in which traditional drama, far from being "natural," is a construct reflecting a falsely soothing, inherently reactionary view of life. This kind of argument is familiar to those aware of avant-garde theory in general, and of recent theories of deconstruction, distancing of audience from text, and elimination of pleasure-giving elements in narrative as strategies for allowing readers/viewers to free themselves of the reactionary pull of bourgeois narrative.

In practice, of course, producers of alternative media most commonly use these very techniques as a means of wrenching audiences from their complacent, pleasurable involvement in traditional, most often popular, narrative. Whether they are producing nonrealist narratives or artworks, or documentaries that seek to deconstruct the mainstream media presentations of political or social events, the intent is the same. The camera is a visible presence. The process of creating the work, of sifting through myriad contradictory perspectives and creating a montage of incompatible, irreconcilable versions of reality is foregrounded. The viewer is thus presumed to leave the viewing experience in a state of confusion and questioning that is seen as an intellectually active, involved one, as opposed to the nursery-pudding comfort of traditional realist drama, no matter how "radical" in intent.

The responses to these views, as presented in a series of *Screen* magazine articles, raise a variety of questions. Some authors simply disagree with MacCabe and defend realism's potential to produce radical changes in a viewer's feelings and beliefs. Others are more conflicted, seeing the merit in MacCabe's position but also defending at least some aspects of realistic drama like *Days of Hope* and other similar British TV docudramas. Colin McArthur, for example, insists that *Days of Hope* does handle contradiction in certain key scenes in which the dominant discourse of the time is called into question by key characters (1981, 304). He suggests that we think not of a single, unitary "realism," but of a variety of "realisms," some reactionary and some not, the test being "the extent to which its formal strategies mark a departure from the dominant film and television discourses of [the] society" (309). McArthur also refers to the importance, seen by the producers of *Days of Hope*, of using familiar narrative forms in order to reach a wider audience than is reached by the kind of nonrealist work MacCabe and many artists insist is the only politically progressive project.

John Caughie, in his intervention in the debate, raises another important issue: the differences between what he calls "the American factions" of docudrama, seen in works like *Holocaust* and *Washington: Behind Closed Doors*, which do in fact follow very traditional, "transparent" strategies and others, such as *Days of Hope*, that use what he calls "a documentary style" that has a certain look as a result of specific camera, lighting, and acting techniques (Caughie 1981, 327–52). For our purposes, the question of acting is irrelevant since all telefeatures on American television follow the classic style. Documentary, on the other hand, which involves the clear presence of a journalist/narrator, is comparable to the *Days of Hope* example. This is why I felt it was important here to look at an actual American documentary. We do not make "documentary-style" dramas for network television. Caughie, in any event, makes a strong case for naturalism by insisting, quite rightly, that it is "in any kind of historical sense . . . something more than a form, a mere absence of style." Further, he says, naturalism "has served within a politics of radical humanism to introduce into the social discourses . . . in certain points in history an element (the working class, women, social justice) which had previously been excluded" (338).

Two other media analysts, Douglas Kellner in this country and Raymond Williams, most significantly, in Britain, have further found reasons to defend realism politically. In an influential article written in 1978, Kellner argued that in spite of American television's obviously conservative agenda and its related conservative system of narrative and codes, it nonetheless allowed for occasional, significant moments of emancipatory vision (Kellner 1978, 482). Using a Gramscian model of the inherent contradictions in all dominant ideologies, Kellner saw the possibility of creating within a dominant discourse contradictory, sometimes radical, elements that might indeed be unsettling to viewers.

Williams, writing more recently, retains his long-standing defense of realism as a possible strategy for creating oppositional moments, or perhaps more than moments, within popular realist forms. He speaks of popular TV drama as a mixed bag, of course. But, interestingly, he raises the matter of gossip—surely a major pull for American viewers—as in some cases touching on serious social matters. "There are," he says, "human interests in what happens next to people which are often low order gossip interests, but some are rather high order interests" (Williams 1980, 6–7). It is these high-order gossip interests that I believe need to be addressed and defended in looking at TV movies that—as the ones I am about to analyze do—actually work in politically interesting, sometimes transgressive ways.

Before getting to the films themselves, however, there is another matter that is crucial to this theoretical introduction: the question of reader response and involvement in the production of texts. What MacCabe and the others, no matter what their position in the debate, ignore is what John Fiske calls "the nature of the viewing process by which sense is made of both the program and the viewer." Fiske insists—and I know this to be true from my own experience as a viewer and a teacher—that viewers do in fact "bring extra-textual experience and attitudes to bear upon the reading of the text." Both MacCabe and McArthur deny this ability and freedom, even in a limited sense. They work with a model that, not unlike the hypodermic theorists, who assume we receive messages from television passively, gives far more power to the text to influence belief and behavior than more recent thinking, happily, suggests it has. Again, referring to a Gramscian model, Fiske describes hegemony as "constant struggle against a multitude of resistances to ideological domination" and says that "any balance of forces it achieves is always precarious, always in need of reachievement." Moreover, he says, any society "will evidence numerous points where subordinate groups have resisted the total domination that is the aim of hegemony and have withheld their consent to the system" (Fiske 1987, 39–41). It is in this context that we need to view American telefeatures. But first, a brief excursion into alternative forms.

Alternative Video, Realism, and Narrative Strategy

Who Killed Vincent Chin? is a brilliantly executed, culturally and politically sophisticated look at the events that led to a young Chinese-American engineer's being bludgeoned to death by a white man and his son who were tried twice but never convicted of any crime. Set in Detroit, at a time when the auto industry was collapsing and anti-Japanese feelings ran high, it does several things TV movies do not do. Substantively, it places the incident in a broad, complex socioeconomic context in which issues of race, class, and capitalism figure largely and explicitly. Ron Ebens, the murderer, was—or had been—a highly paid industry executive. His luxurious life included an elegant home and a social life that revolved around country clubs and a circle of equally privileged friends and colleagues. When the crash came, he lost his job. One night, in a seedy club where he went to drink and watch the "exotic dancers," he became involved in an altercation with

Chin, himself at a kind of stag party on the eve of his marriage. The evening ended with Chin's death: he was battered with a baseball bat.

While the extensive, often contradictory testimony of myriad witnesses gives a variety of versions of the event itself, the narrative structure of the documentary leads inexorably to a clear and biased interpretation: Chin, mistaken for Japanese, was a scapegoat for white rage at Japanese imports seen—largely because of industry and media propaganda—as the cause of Detroit's decline.

I raise this structural issue because, in spite of the apparently "objective" and complex techniques employed by the video-makers, the fact is that, like traditional Hollywood narrative, this work leads the viewer to a very pointed, unavoidable conclusion about right and wrong, justice and injustice, and, indeed, racism and capitalism. The point of view is overridingly that of the producers themselves. While the testimonies conflict, the narrative line becomes increasingly unambiguous and one-sided. After a local jury acquits, the Asian community mobilizes an effective media campaign that—through some legal technicalities—results in a new trial in another state. Again, the verdict is acquittal. If the Detroit populace is too emotionally involved to be fair, the new jury—totally uninvolved in the race and class issues at the root of the case—still fails to see, and in this case care much about, the racial injustice done to an innocent man and his family. In this sense, the audience is not, as the antirealists argue, left with troubling questions and a possible incentive to become involved in the issues. On the contrary, the viewer knows full well, by tape's end, what has happened, and why and what to feel about it— outrage. The formal properties of the documentary, then, radically different as they are from standard TV docudrama, nonetheless work toward the same kind of narrative and ideological closure.

Looking at the technical aspects of the videotape, we find much more that is arguably "radical" in substance and, if not in any way that is demonstrably and unambiguously clear, in its effect on viewers. I am not, in any sense, disparaging this work. On the contrary, I think it is an extraordinary piece of video journalism. I would not wish to see such alternative works disappear since they have an important role to play in the larger realm of public discourse. The point I stress is twofold: first, what it does well can be done only in the context of a limited, highly selective audience, and second, for all its artistic virtue it is no less structured to achieve a preordained response from the viewer—except in the kinds of negotiated readings Fiske refers to—than TV movies. There is a preferred reading and a dominant text here just as there is in commercial media.

So what does the film do technically and artistically? First, as Colin McArthur argues, it insists on calling attention to its own televisual apparatus (1981, 306). The trappings of the documentary style (in *Days of Hope* used in a dramatization of events of a kind not produced in this country) are inescapable. Witnesses appear as talking heads answering questions posed by a filmmaker whose presence is always apparent, even when she is not visible. The piece is grainy, vérité, poorly lit, and totally devoid of the slick production values typical of commercial television. In particular, the mise-en-scène is calculated to impress upon viewers the "unstaged" quality of the content. Interviews, city shots, and news clips all suggest that someone has captured, in a way very different from the "naturalness" and "transparency" so abhorred by MacCabe in traditional drama, an authentic slice of life. The documentary seems to present a complex reality from not one but several subject positions, all of which are in some sense valid and respected. That this multiplicity of viewpoints, this lack of ideological closure is in fact betrayed by the narrative structure of the work is significant, however. Far from leaving the conscientious viewer with a sense of questioning, a demand for a certain level of intellectual work on the issues raised, the tape has as clear an agenda as any TV movie; it is simply produced in a more ideologically and artistically interesting—or at least more sophisticated—fashion.

What is actually different about this documentary, what most separates it from mainstream narrative, is its mosaic of elements, its multiplicity of styles and materials, all of which do work to disengage viewers from easy identification with and involvement in the personal stories and force them to focus on a variety of more abstract concerns. Structurally, the tape is fragmented. It jumps from interview to interview, from clips of cultural elements of Detroit—most notably musical performances, ranging from Motown to chauvinistic (if wistful) public performances of the "Detroit will rise again" variety—to long shots of city streets, to scenes that contrast the cultural life of the Chinese immigrants with that of the white managerial classes, to clips of local and national news reports and even a "Donahue" show featuring the victim's mother.

Among the most moving of the atmospheric cultural scenes are those in which Mrs. Chin describes her difficulties in adjusting to American life and her pride in her son and those that show hate-filled events such as the demolition derbies in which a group of raging whites gleefully and vengefully demolish a series of Japanese cars as massive crowds look on and cheer. But these brief moments of near-melodrama and passion are quickly undercut by the quick cuts to other matters and other modes of presentation. We do not become absorbed or emotionally identified, even with Mrs. Chin, because she is not a character in the dramatic sense, but a witness giving testimony, as in a trial. We do not, as is standard in TV movies, see her as a roundly drawn character over a period of time. Moreover, her suffering is presented in a context that has no stylistic or personal connection to her immediate situation. There are, for example, fragments that document the economic decline of the Motor City as reported by the media, and there are bits that link this decline to a growing climate of racist hatred of Asian-Americans generally, although of course it is Japan that is the actual target.

What is commendable and moving here—and quite different from standard TV narrative—is the complex analysis of the various forces at work in Detroit that combined to make inevitable a violent clash that the Chin murder represents only as an emblematic and dramatic case. The producers do force us to see this dramatic story in terms that are ultimately and utterly cultural, political, and economic. Unlike TV moviemakers, they transcend the personal drama and focus almost exclusively on the larger context. We do not become emotionally involved with Mrs. Chin's agony except in a superficial way. She is simply one of many people interviewed, all of whom are hurting for reasons that can only be understood in terms of political analysis.

It would be going too far to say that the producers allow us to feel sympathy for the Eben family. Nonetheless, neither they nor others are presented as vicious brutes, but rather as people sunk in their subjectivity and cultural isolation who are reacting to capitalistic forces that have victimized them in the same way they have victimized everyone else in the documentary. In that sense, the piece does work to deconstruct systemic forces largely invisible to those of us who live in, or watch commercial programs about, the events at hand: murder, American economic processes, cultural conflicts between different sorts of people.

Still, can we say that this film has done more than—or even as much as—the movies we are about to examine to change consciousness? There are many reasons why I think not. First, its venue—alternative media outlets and public television stations—attracts audiences who already agree with its premise and in many cases already understand the more subtle political issues raised. People who do not fit this category rarely seek out films like this. This is not to say that they are not valuable. Some people certainly will see a film like this and be "educated" and perhaps changed by it. I have used it in my classes precisely to emphasize the differences and strengths of alternative, engaged media.

My (largely working-class) students' responses to the film are interesting. While they are moved by what is to them a new perspective, they nonetheless find it more difficult to watch and become involved in. They are a captive audience, of course, and this viewing experience for the most part does not lead to an interest in seeing more documentary works. For one thing, the structure and the ideological underpinnings demand a lot of close attention and thought, something all but the most serious students in the best universities rarely are willing to engage in. In other words, the classroom experience doesn't translate into their lives. They would rather watch *Roots*. This reality undercuts MacCabe's idealist belief in the political impact of avant-garde, as opposed to popular, texts. To the extent that we know how audiences respond to texts, and what, in the long run, they do with them, there is no reason to think this kind of alternative medium moves people to change or action more than popular forms do. In fact, there may be more evidence that TV movies have a better chance of doing that than the avant-gardists realize.

129

Roots: History As Melodrama

The impact of *Roots*, the 1976 miniseries that ran for eight consecutive nights and garnered unprecedented and unanticipated ratings, is by now a matter of record. The series, based on the Alex Haley book that documented the history—a mythologized history, but one based on a good deal of previously unfamilar fact about the black experience in this country—was a media event that certainly entered the public sphere and changed the terms of discourse about race as well as American history forever. To a generation unfamiliar with black history, a subject certainly not then taught in schools, the series was an eye opener, not least because it presented history solely through the eyes of an oppressed minority—a technique unheard of until then.

The series, according to Nielsen, drew 130 million viewers for at least part of its twelve-hour run. The final episode drew an amazing 80 million viewers, surpassing *Gone with the Wind* and all eleven Super Bowls to become the highest rated TV show ever. (Fishbein 1983, 281). No affiliate, north or south, rejected it, and more than 250 colleges and universities offered courses based on the series and the book (Fishbein 1983, 294)—this in spite of the fact that all the heroes were black and most of the villains white. As one would expect, given the importance of what Fiske calls "extra-textual materials" that viewers bring to viewing and that enter into viewer response, those most positively affected tended to be more liberal to begin with. Still, other sources suggest more subtle, long-term effects. For example, in a telephone interview with 971 viewers of both races, the predominant emotion expressed was neither guilt nor increased anger and hostility but rather sadness (Fishbein 1983, 282). To the extent that such studies indicate anything clear and substantial, they probably show that people were simply moved by the drama in a deep way. I would argue, however, that in the long run it is just such an emotional impact that stays with one and colors the way one experiences and responds to certain kinds of events—in this case racial events—subtly but meaningfully.

Few people, especially those who were then children, fail to have vivid memories of watching the series. (I have never had a student, for example, who did not remember, often in vivid detail, the series as a whole and certain key scenes especially.) Whatever viewers brought to the series in the way of extratextual attitudes and experiences, it is clear that *Roots* became a part of the extratextual material with which they viewed and negotiated future textual readings and (probably) real-life experiences. In other words, the process of negotiation of textual readings, while important in initial responses to the series, may well be even more important in readings of other texts, later in life.

Nor does a negotiated reading exist in an asocial vacuum. That *Roots* was in fact a national media event of enormous impact, that it was a shared experience for an entire nation, talked about and analyzed in everyone's personal and social life, is the key to its enduring effect on attitudes. This is exactly what alternative media, no matter how ideologically or artistically more sophisticated, simply cannot achieve. For all its failings and ideological contradictions and limits, *Roots* changed a nation's way of seeing and feeling about racial issues.

Dramatically, the secret of *Roots*'s success was its clever management of the generic form as it had developed over a decade of TV movie production. As we have seen, this set of conventions was largely a function of fitting dramatic elements into a master plan preordained by the commercial and, to a lesser extent, the political needs and constraints of network television. As Leslie Fishbein has pointed out, the "craftsmanship of its structure" was a key element in its appeal to viewers. Unlike documentaries like *Who Killed Vincent Chin?*, which—as is appropriate—reveal negative aspects of the American system and present to a public not necessarily aware of them gross miscarriages of justice that are not redressed, *Roots* is unrelentingly upbeat in its narrative strategy. Every episode, no matter how grotesque its substance, how appalling its revelations about American racism and the brutality of whites against blacks, invariably ends on a positive note. There is always some significant triumph in the concluding segments (Fishbein 1983, 283).

The second installment—the one we will look at in some detail—for example, centers on the relationship between Fiddler, a "house nigger" canny in his ability to garner certain privileges and comforts by doing his plantation owner/master's bidding, and Kunta Kinte, a rebellious new slave he is charged to train and to break spiritually. Kinte endures the most excruciating humiliation and physical torture but refuses to give in. Specifically, he refuses, even under the whip, to accept his slave name, Toby, and insists—broken, bleeding, and possibly near death—that his name is Kunta Kinte.

Fiddler gradually comes to admire Kunta and feel close to him. He tries to reason with his charge because, of course, his own material position depends upon his success in breaking Kunta. As he watches the flogging and is deeply disturbed by it, Fiddler makes a final attempt to negotiate with his master by arguing economics. "You got an investment here," he tells the owner, and "ruining him" will mean the loss of that investment. Failing in this effort, he finally takes a side and stand, becoming a man who—for the first time—sees his own position and its privileges as unimportant in relation to the far nobler struggle of his friend for dignity and freedom. The final scene in this episode is an affirmation of hope and solidarity. Holding the nearly dead hero, his face a study of anger and sorrow of an intensity heretofore unknown to the carefree opportunist, Fiddler vows, as tears stream from his eyes, that "There gonna be another day!"

This brief description of the second episode points to the, literally, made-for-TV methods of the producers. The segment is dramatically self-contained and uplifting in its resolution. It also contains—as does the series as a whole—an enormous amount of sheer sensational violence, brutality, and melodrama. Subplots involve the sexual exploitation of young female slaves; it is brutal and inhuman, but nonetheless sexual (if not sexy). It demands and skillfully maneuvers audience involvement of a deeply personal emotional kind. We see two central characters change, and we witness an enormously moving process of bonding between them that is both personal and political. Audiences came back for more because they were increasingly involved with characters and because the action was so very sensational and dramatic.

Unlike *Vincent Chin*, *Roots* does not reach beyond the personal to place its story in a complex political context that pushes the boundaries of mainstream TV (Foner 1977, 263–64). It is primarily a moral tale, and its ideology, as should be no surprise, is rooted in family values. Others have observed that *Roots* was most profoundly "mythological" in its inspiring, but not entirely accurate, presentation of slavery as a system that sought to destroy families and of the slave community managing to combat that attempt and keep its family structure intact. Later episodes show how important this theme is to the series. The key players do end up successful and materially prosperous. More importantly, though, this success is always understood in terms of family values. The ex-slaves of *Roots* are presented as very much like other immigrant cultures in their concern for family and for achieving the American Dream, in the interest of giving their children a good life and seeing them become more successful than their parents.

This is not to say that ideological issues do not come up. Actually, the discourses of racism play a prominent role in the series, as does the capitalist profit motive in the system of slavery. Mr. Reynolds, the not-entirely-bad plantation owner, for example, has lengthy discussions with his far more purely racist manager and with his more liberal, though certainly less confident, wife about the doctrine of racial inferiority upon which slavery rests. At one point she hesitantly asks her husband why, if blacks are genetically inferior to begin with, he should fear the results of educating them.

This, however, is fairly obvious stuff and it is certainly overshadowed by the far more moving dramatic scenes of brutality, humiliation, love, and struggle. This is what gets ratings, after all, and this is also what will pass muster with network executives and sponsors who avoid talky, much less intellectually challenging or oppositional, elements. *Roots* is a safe series. It only says what everyone who lived through the civil rights movement already knew. It does not challenge basic institutions as does *Vincent Chin*. On the contrary, it ultimately insists that the American Dream works if you just keep your family first in your heart and work hard and believe in yourself. I need not enumerate all the political contradictions and loopholes in that particular approach to American society, then or now.

Looking more closely at the text as a dramatic and technical work, we see more clearly how the series actually worked aesthetically. To begin with, while the cast was predominantly black, the producers were quick to ensure that big names—some black but most white—appeared in the series, often in cameo roles. The star system was crucial to its success. Actors included Ed Asner, Lorne Greene, Sandy Duncan, Leslie Uggams, Lloyd Bridges,

Chuck Connors, Ben Vereen, and others who were quite prominent at the time.

More interestingly, the producers got around the problem of presenting a series entirely from the black perspective by using certain television techniques so effectively that white audiences were drawn into identification with subjects heretofore seen exclusively, in popular drama, as Other. The use of close-ups and two shots, emphasizing emotional reaction and response, is the most obvious and effective of these.

Kunta Kinte is always the principal subject. In a reversal of pop culture conventions for portraying white/black and white/Native American relations, *Roots* manages to make the whites, with whom audiences have been taught to identify in history texts as well as media texts, appear very clearly as secondary. They are, at last, presented as Other. In the scene in which Kunta and the friends he has made on the slave ship are auctioned off, for example, the authority of the wealthy, powerful, confident white men is masterfully subverted by the fact that Kunta is the reference point for interpreting events.

The technique by which this is accomplished is typically televisual. Everything that happens is presented in brief segments, always interrupted by cuts to Kunta's expressive face. He registers a vast array of intense emotional responses. When a friend is bought by a man who tells the auctioneer leeringly that the exchange has been "my pleasure, and I anticipate she *will* be my pleasure," he is viewed in terms of the black response. The young woman herself expresses sheer terror and humiliation, but Kunta's face is a study in absolute rage and indignation. These close-ups, which involve little or no dialogue since the slaves do not at first speak or understand English and later are severely restricted in what they are allowed to say, are nonetheless the dominant dramatic element in the series. The preferred text is their text, the subordinate readings—for a refreshing change—must be negotiated by, one assumes, a segment of the audience that is extreme in its racism and brings to the viewing experience some very strong extratextual beliefs. The good guy/bad guy conventions of pop culture have simply been turned on their heads.

The historical accuracy of this series, as I have said, is always questionable. In fact, historical inaccuracies abound and have been documented extensively (Fishbein 1983, 289). In this, the series is wholly different from *Vincent Chin* and has very different goals. Haley himself has attributed the drama's success to "the average American's yearning for a sense of heritage" and insisted that this yearning crosses race lines and reflects "a universal concern with family, lineage, and ancestry shared by every person on earth" (in Gerber 1977, 87). James Monaco has further noted that "Black Americans are not alone in their search for ethnic roots and it seems likely that millions of white viewers were attracted as much by the saga of immigration and assimilation as by racial politics" (Monaco 1978, 159).

The failure to show how the realities of black history are different from most other immigrant histories is one of the contradictions of the series. It works because it twists itself into the genre of family I discussed in detail in the preceding chapters. Above all, it is a classic TV movie. But it is also something far more daring and socially significant. It flies in the face of avant-garde notions of the wholly reactionary nature of traditional realist drama in numerous ways. Its impact, its message, its role in the public sphere, and its staying power as an event in history, shared by a nation and discussed endlessly not only in personal discourse but all over the media, based as they are on melodramatic shtick, are not in the long run reactionary. It is certainly not "revolutionary," to use MacCabe's grandiose term, but it is, I think, presumptuous, and even naive, to assume that media products in and of themselves could ever be primary agents of revolution, even in those heady days when the word could be used and discussed seriously. The media exist within a larger social context. They are only one element in any social process and cannot bear the burden of converting people. *Roots*—especially seen fifteen years after it aired—is, like *Kent State*, a surprisingly powerful and effective experience that has aged very well indeed.

Crisis at Central High:
History and Race As Women's Issue

To move from *Roots* to a discussion of *Crisis at Central High*, a far more traditional example of the treatment of race and history

in TV movies, is in many ways anticlimactic. This movie, powerful in its own way, is very much in the tradition of the films we
discussed in the last chapter. A docudrama about the historic battle for integration in Little Rock, Arkansas, its center is yet another
strong, principled, nurturing white woman. Joanne Woodward
plays Elizabeth Huckaby, a teacher at Central High in 1957, the
year when blacks first entered the formerly all white school.

Huckaby, and the perspective of her journal (upon which the
film is based), are ready-made for the genre. In the opening voice-
over narration, she explains that her story is "a journal of a year,"
that its concern is "not why but what," and that her primary interest is to tell "the story of the children" who were affected by
the historic events. Nothing could be more conventional.

Add to this the presentation of Huckaby's life and character, the
changes she goes through, and her identity as a "polite" (to use
her word), genteel southern white "lady," and you clearly have
a middle-class white perspective. There is no doubt that the
blacks are represented as Other. Nor is there any doubt that Huckaby, a childless, aging woman, sees herself as a kind of surrogate
mother, not, by any means, an activist. Toward the end of the
story, she tells her husband that a significant element of her experience was that "I came as close as I ever have to feeling like
a mother."

In essence then this is a history lesson in which the definition
of the traditional American family is expanded to include black as
well as white children. The "family" in question is a school family. It is, as we have seen, the way of TV movies to translate everything into familial terms, to reduce social and political issues to exclusively personal, emotional ones. Indeed, in one of the film's
occasional narrative voice-overs, Huckaby comments that "the
Russians sent Sputnik into space and for a few brief days the nation looked away from us and toward the sky. But for the Negro
children each day was a small war."

This kind of exposition serves to blot out the larger world context in which the story occurs and that ultimately must be understood in order for it to make full sense. It insists that the children's
"small wars" be defined emotionally and personally and that all
other aspects of the political climate of the United States in the fifties be seen as irrelevant. In comparison, *Roots*, with its refer-

ences to capitalism, imperialism, and racial ideologies—no matter how unrevolutionary they may seem to Marxist scholars—stands out as a veritable left-wing political tract.

That *Central High* is in fact far more representative of TV's way of handling both race and history makes it important to our discussion, of course. That it is also, for many reasons, a particularly affecting and intelligent example of the form makes this even more true. Once more we are in pursuit of a theory, a rationale, for taking seriously an admittedly limited and in many ways politically inadequate form of discourse. Since we have already discussed so many similar films, the discussion need not be as extensive as those of *Roots* or *Executioner's Song*.

What is exemplary here is the character of Huckaby, a traditional woman who is seen to grow and change when she is faced with an ordeal that is also a challenge. Huckaby is no Lois Gibbs. She is a southern lady of the 1950s, a time when activism, even in the more liberal north, was unheard of. It is therefore not surprising that the heroine never sees herself or her options in more radical terms. Her integrity, her strength, and her infinite fairness are for this reason all the more remarkable.

At first determined simply to obey the law, she gradually develops a commitment to her mission: to ensure equal education to "Negroes" because she comes to know her particular students and care for them. When she is told by her husband (whose role is small but supportive) that she is overwrought because she is personalizing the situation and that she should consider taking a sabbatical, she replies, "Maybe it's time I personalize. I've never joined a club, never signed a petition. Maybe it's time I took a sabbatical from that."

In the course of the drama we see her change, not dramatically but impressively, from someone who is deferentially feminine to a fault into someone who, while always the well-mannered lady, stands up unflinchingly to abuse, social ostracism, and incredible stress. When the National Guard arrives to keep the blacks out of school, she nearly simpers. Offered a ride through the guarded gates, which no blacks are allowed to pass through, she says girlishly, "Oh, thank you. I've never ridden in a jeep before." And when disgruntled white students express unhappiness with the disruptions of their normal lives she agrees. "Yes," she nods, "I wish things were back to normal too."

She never completely loses this pleasant agreeability. Even toward the end, when a social situation in her home evolves into a racist diatribe directed against her by an old friend, she does not lose her temper or even assert her own views. She simply ends the evening early and says to her husband, "I don't know why I'm so polite."

To the extent that Huckaby is an exemplary figure it is always because of her rising to an occasion *in spite of* her social position and her stereotypically feminine personality. She never becomes anything but what she is—a southern lady. But in historic terms, she behaves in ways most of her sex and class do not and cannot. This construction is of course determined in great part by the demands of the networks. This is no *Roots*. It involved neither the risk nor the possibility of doing something historically unique that characterized that much-discussed series. The producers, Richard Levinson and William Link, surely had an easier time "pitching" *Central High* than the producers pitching *Roots*. After all, it fit perfectly into the generic conventions. Its historic or political message—twenty years after the events it recounted—was by the 1970s very tame indeed. Nor did the film attempt to push the limits of the form either in political content or in dramatic conventions.

So, once again, we are back to our original argument: that TV films, seen largely by women viewers and by a general audience not familiar with even those details of the historic event allowed by the constrained perspective, become a part of the national consciousness and public discourse; that they do, to some extent, redefine the construct of womanhood and of citizenship; and that they do these things in terms that are not so heroic as to put off mainstream viewers. The contradictions are obvious. Watching *Central High* is often frustrating. One wants to shake Huckaby for being so damned nice, so *un*political in her approach. It is not enough, by feminist and left standards. But there are moments of transcendence here as well, moments of small but nonetheless heroic actions. Within the confines of the dominant hegemonic discourse, a challenge is taken up and a triumph observed. The film illustrates what one very ordinary person who is very much a part of the oppressive culture she inhabits can do in extremely unthreatening ways. It need not be belabored that this element of transgression, these moments of resistance to the status quo and glimpses of a utopian resolution to racial discord, could not possibly be achieved in any but traditionally realist form. Yes, certainly, the status quo is largely preserved. The idea that institutions and ideologies can accommodate significant social change is reinforced, not challenged. Nonetheless, I am not at all convinced that that is the main issue here. The engagement of audiences and the intermittent moments of resistance that can occur in a mass media production deserve to be analyzed far more respectfully than left-wing purists believe.

The Executioner's Song: Class and the Networks

In discussing the presentation of race in TV movies, we were dealing with clear ideological constructs and discourses. Race, like sex, is well understood as a hot political issue of great import—whether from the perspective of justice or of reactionary fear and hatred—in which every American is consciously engaged from a very young age. With class, the situation is quite the opposite. Most TV movies do not deal with working-class issues or characters. In those rare exceptions where they do, the perspective, as we saw in our discussions of *The Burning Bed*, *Silent Witness*, and *Lois Gibbs* (all, not incidentally, produced by the same man, Robert Greenwald) is implicitly middle-class anyway. "Good" working-class people aspire to and achieve middle-class lives and values. If that aspect of their lives does not change, it is simply because they already live in terms of middle-class values and lifestyles, particulary those that center on the traditional nuclear family as the norm for a good life.

There are, however, occasional features that do present working-class life as a given and focus on the lives of poor, "uncultivated" characters on their own terms, or at least the terms in which the network producers see them. These films do not end with the protagonists being saved and transcending their roots. They end, typically, in tragedy. Moreover, everything about these films—style, mise-en-scène, characterization, narrative strategy—

139

is dramatically different from the movies we have looked at so far. Like their central figures, they are different, a minor breed—in effect, a subgenre.

It is an interesting historic fact that the few movies that fit this subgenre have been produced quite recently, in the mid- to late eighties. The shifts in dominant theme and style that can be charted historically, even in the brief two decades in which TV movies have been produced, will be examined in the afterword. For our purposes here, I want only to look at representational and ideological issues raised in the presentation of class, particularly in films that, like the others we have analyzed in this chapter, portray actual events of historic significance.

I chose *The Executioner's Song* for several reasons. For one thing, its production values and script are not only different from the classic TV movie but far more sophisticated. Based on Norman Mailer's book of the same name, and written by Mailer himself, it passes muster—for all but the most hard-core critics of television and mass culture—as serious "art." In fact, in Europe, it ran in movie theaters rather than on television and was critically very well received (Rapping 1987, 145). This is a common occurrence, actually. The Europeans have not been involved in the peculiarly American arguments about high/low, mass/avant-garde art—at least in regard to our media, which they have always appreciated. In our country there is still a virulent contempt for network television. Theorists, critics, and intellectuals have only recently, and in limited numbers, begun to reevaluate this stance. That this is the first serious, respectful study of TV movies is testimony to this intellectual blind spot, which is not shared by the highly sophisticated French critical establishment.

In any event, *Executioner's Song* is a work deserving of serious regard. In a pool of so few TV movies treating class, it is the one that best expresses the ideological tensions surrounding this subject—the condition that dare not speak its name—as seen by the mainstream media. Other examples—*I Know My First Name Is Steven* is a notable one—are not only few and far between, but are also far less interesting. What they have in common is a view of the working class, or more typically perhaps the underclass, as inherently "different from you and me," as Scott Fitzgerald said to Ernest Hemingway about "the very rich." To the extent that poor people refuse, or fail, to strive for or achieve a middle-class life, they are portrayed as—almost—genetically deficient. But where such a representation of blacks would be unthinkable because of the widespread understanding of racist ideology, in these films the message, perhaps subtle but equally odious, goes down quite easily, mostly because the public realm does not include a common discourse on class.

Executioner's Song is the story of Gary Gilmore, a sociopathic criminal who finally admits that he is "evil" and deserves to die for his crimes, which are certainly inhuman and brutal. He finds love, for the first time, with a young woman—she is nineteen, he is thirty-five—as spiritually hopeless as he is and a lot less smart and functional. Their relationship is portrayed exclusively in terms of various kinds of animal passion, primarily sexual, of course. Nicole Baker is a young mother who has been institutionalized, and abused, because of mental instability. She has several marriages and a string of lovers behind her and is presented as a sexual provocateur.

For his part, Gilmore is a hothead and a cynic whose years in prison for various crimes have left him hardened and crude. He eats with his fingers, has no social graces, and antagonizes everyone in his orbit. Both Gilmore and Baker are chronically depressed and self-destructive. Both use drugs and sex in excess, to say the least, according to middle-class TV standards. Gilmore also has a hot temper and an apparently uncontrollable need to grab what he wants at the moment he wants it. He craves instant gratification and goes into a rage when he is thwarted. In one scene, for example, he goes out with a woman his cousin has set him up with. When his advances are rebuffed by the woman, who tells him "You can't have everything in five minutes," he is furious and seems on the brink of violence. "You want to hit me, don't you?" says the disgusted woman.

In many ways this scene, and this character, are reminiscent of Travis Bickle in Martin Scorsese's *Taxi Driver*. But that theatrical film succeeded in presenting its main character in a social context and in making him a sympathetic character simply because, throughout his bizarre meanderings, he is clearly driven by a desire—misguided, of course—to help a young prostitute and an even more poignant desire to establish a relationship with a classy, beautiful woman whose middle-class life and work intrigue him. Gilmore is a different fish entirely. He has no altruistic dreams, nor does he wish to rise above his own station, which he accepts as his natural milieu. He is actually "saner" than Bickle, but, for most of the film, almost wholly lacking in sympathetic qualities.

Executioner's Song also differs dramatically from *Taxi Driver* in its adherence to certain TV movie norms about family, responsibility, and fitting into a community. Gilmore does have a family that cares about him and offers him an alternative to his old life. His uncle gives him a job. His cousin Brenda loves him. They, especially Brenda, serve as the voices of telefeature normality, always trying to save him by integrating him into their lifestyle, which is, as is typical, working class but aspiring to or reflective of middle-class goals and values.

Gilmore is an attractive character but a scary and obnoxious one, too. When he hooks up with Baker it is the blind leading the blind, the loser and misfit finding a soul mate. "I know you from some other life," he tells her early on, and this reference to mystical, decidedly nonrational modes of thought is a sign, heavily coded, that these two are too weird to adjust to the rational, therapeutic world TV movies are almost always rooted in. They are for many reasons beyond the pale from the start, permanent outsiders who cling to each other out of a shared understanding of that fact.

Sex and violence figure very quickly in their doomed relationship. He has a tendency to impotence, which, at one point, he attributes to his years in prison. "I'm not used to sex with women," he remarks. In other words, his life experiences, leading to and culminating in a long prison term, are presented as permanently damaging to his ability to function "normally." When Baker goads and insults him about his sexual inadequacy, at one point suggesting that he "prefers boys," he becomes violent.

As things progress, he returns to violent crime because he wants to buy a truck and cannot wait until he saves the money. He involves her and even her children in his escapades. But what is even more distressing is the way in which the movie portrays the other members of their social circle. Baker's mother actually agrees to store his guns in her house, as though this were a perfectly normal request deserving of assent. When Gilmore's good, quasi-bourgeois relatives ask a friend of Baker's where she might be, after she and Gilmore go off on a crime spree, the young woman replies "I don't even know where my own husband is" and slams the door, as though erratic disappearance were a normal part of life, even married family life.

This is most certainly a grim tale in which no punches are pulled. But at whose expense and to what purpose? If we compare it to the more typical woman-in-danger films and TV movies so common since the seventies we see profound differences. In these films, the victim is invariably an innocent and more than likely a woman of the middle class. In theatrical films, it is the killer who occupies the subject position, in one sense, because the action is seen through his eyes. But it is the victim with whom we identify because we experience her terror and oppression most clearly. Usually, in fact, these B-grade exploitation films do not even portray the stalker visually. He is the driving force of the action but he is nonetheless a nonperson, a mere agent of atrocity. The female victim is the character we relate to. In that sense, it is she who is clearly the subject. The viewer position, then, is ambiguous. Male viewers who are so inclined can vicariously identify with the pathologically misogynist perpetrator. Female and other sympathetic viewers, on the other hand, are invited to identify with the victim.

In TV movies this is usually done differently. Women-in-danger films invariably feature female protagonists who are only temporarily victimized and who, ultimately, rise to the occasion, fight back, and are instrumental in bringing the beast down. The movies about serial rapist/murderer Ted Bundy and movies like *Fatal Vision* and *A Death in Texas* insist on a more "feminist" preferred reading in which victimized women are transformed into victorious actors who transform themselves—much as Elizabeth Huckaby did in *Crisis at Central High*—into strong, confident fighters for justice and for their own self-esteem. This is the utopian element in these often frightening and depressing "based-on-fact" tales. When this does not happen, when the woman is killed, a sister/surrogate often takes up the battle in her name. In movies about prostitutes who are killed, for example, an advocate of some kind, a social worker or lawyer, takes up the struggle.

Daughter of the Streets is one such movie among others too numerous to list (for a full documentation see Marill 1987).

What distinguishes *Executioner's Song* and *I Know My First Name Is Steven* is the lack of both feminist and middle-class perspective. Gilmore's story is exclusively his; his world is exclusively a world of the underclass, with only the barest nod to family and middle-class ideologies. In other words, the film insists on presenting the life of poor people as a self-contained universe that bears little resemblance to the dominant world of prime time.

Artistically, this is the key to the film's extraordinary power. It breaks with TV-movie realism, although it is thoroughly realist— or more accurately naturalist—in its mode of presentation. But its naturalism is lyrical, atmospheric, often oblique in its dialogue in a way that, as we have seen, is contrary to generic norms. Gilmore is presented in very poetic terms. Music—country and rockabilly—creates meaning and elicits feeling. Lengthy (for TV) scenes focus on landscapes and abjure dialogue. We see Gilmore walking down highways in scenes that serve no purpose other than to establish his isolation and spiritual despair. We see him driving through streets that evoke the spiritual and cultural emptiness of the environments in which poor people exist.

Dialogue is at times mysterious and elliptical. Toward the end, after Gilmore has cold-bloodedly murdered several people to get money for his truck, Baker asks, "Are you the devil?" His reply is almost metaphysical: "The devil doesn't feel any love," he tells her, then says that "I am further from God than the devil" and "I know evil very intimately." This kind of thing works two ways. Artistically it makes for impressive, challenging drama. Ideologically, however, it serves to locate people like Gilmore and Baker in an almost biologically determined subspecies that is based on nothing more than their class backgrounds. Unlike Fran Hughes and the other triumphant working-class TV movie heroines, Gilmore and Baker are exempt from the rhetoric of liberal rationalism, from the plodding narratives in which reason and straightforward, economical exposition of causes and events dominate. If they cannot be saved by the bourgeoisie, then they are doomed to some lower, bestial realm of existence in which reason and redemption do not figure much.

By the end of the film, when Gilmore has been jailed and Baker,

144

after attempting suicide, has been institutionalized, there is a sudden intrusion of more traditional liberal discourse. Suddenly, we hear Gilmore explaining, in traditional telefeature fashion, why he is the way he is. While he insists that "I'm a bad man . . . I truly deserve to die," he also explains his condition quite rationally and in sociological terms: "I'm so used to fear, hate, cheating, distrust, it's my natural habitat. I truly belong in a place like this, dank and dirty."

When the lawyers and journalists come on the scene, the discourse moves—if only briefly—to even more traditional terms. The liberal lawyer who defends Gilmore says in a press interview, for example, that his fate is directly related to the prison system and even to the values of capitalist society. The lawyer criticizes the prison system for locking people up and depriving them of autonomy and of responsibility for themselves. Then he suggests that by throwing these helpless, militaristically disciplined men into a capitalist world based on values that encourage greed and instant gratification and demand self-sufficiency in the rugged individualist mode, the system doubly disables and destroys them. This brief scene, hardly dominant, attacks capitalism on two counts: it socializes us to conform and obey and at the same time contradictorily insists that we compete, achieve, and accumulate, by any means possible.

If, as Fiske argues, "narrative realism makes sense of capitalist society" (1987, 167), this scene is a key element in understanding its strategy. Soon after, Gilmore himself adds to the critique. He tells reporters that he prefers death to prison not simply because he accepts his own "evil" nature, but also because he knows how the prison system uses behavior modification to keep prisoners in line and has seen "the things governments do to people." By film's end there is an element of heroism in this pathetic and abhorrent man. He stands on principle, accepts responsibility, and refuses to die or be destroyed in any way that is not his own choosing. It is a starkly moving, even riveting finale.

On another level, however, it takes a historic event—Gilmore had become, in his own words, "the best known convict in the United States"—and presents it in terms of an implicit class ideology that at times veers dangerously close to fascist. The film is a tragedy because Gilmore is beyond redemption, incapable of change. His deeds, and his pathologically amoral attitude toward them, are never—or only briefly and superficially—explained or socially rationalized. He is, as he says, an evil man. And he is evil in a way that middle-class villains in TV movies never are. Incest perpetrators, alcoholics who abuse their families, men who commit violence against wives and children, all these types are presented as salvageable, forgivable. All are seen, in final scenes, broken and repentant. Not Gary Gilmore. We may find him admirable in his honesty, even in limited ways capable of fleeting feelings toward others. But we are hard pressed to escape the overall picture of a "bad" man who deserves to die. His cousin Brenda tells him, even as she sobs for him, that he is ultimately a "a scum-sucking pig." And even his wistful statement to the press that he would "rather be remembered for [his] humanitarianism and intellect" rings hollow in the light of his refusal to accept the dominant network ideological framework that insists that change is possible, that the worst characters can become useful, stable citizens.

In the end, then, we are left with a puzzle. When TV movies do their best artistic work, they very often do it in terms of a social and human cynicism more typical of serious theatrical films. When they insist on presenting more positive, progressive narratives, they invariably revert to the formulaic, contradictory, and intellectually and emotionally limited terms of the most traditional pop realism. This is not an aesthetically built-in feature of video, of course. It is instead a reflection of dominant thinking—or feeling, actually—about disturbing matters of class in this country.

Afterword

We have looked at the world of TV movies as though they existed to a great extent outside of history. Having constructed a narrative of how they developed as a form, we then spent a great deal of time analyzing various subgenres. But of course, the social world that TV movies seek to represent, and the industrial one in which they are produced, are always changing. I have argued that TV movies about women and the family have, more than other forms, worked in progressive ways to articulate versions of our experiences, not only as women but as blacks and at times as working people, sympathetically.

In the days since *Brian's Song* was aired, however, the political world in which we live has changed dramatically. As I write, the two most liberal Supreme Court justices have resigned, and we face the very real possibility that the right to legal abortion may soon be lost to women in the United States. The tenor of the times is conservative, and the values that have found space in so many of the movies I have analyzed are more oppositional to the dominant culture than they have been since the 1950s.

The nature of television itself has changed dramatically with the rise of cable and video rentals. The networks, upon which all the movies I have discussed were aired, and prime-time television itself—in the period in which television has most existed as a public sphere—have lost much of their centrality. Today, we tape shows for future, private airing, making individual experiences of television more common. More and more people do not watch network television much at all because so many media options exist. Indeed, it is quite common for younger people to be unaware of the difference between made-for-TV and theatrical films. (This is one reason why I decided to write this book.) This confusion is unavoidable now that cable channels and mainstream movie channels like HBO are producing their own made-for-TV features to supplement the stock of theatricals they run. While these movies may sometimes have social agendas, they are not publicized the way the network "specials" are, and they are not received in the same way as a miniseries like *Roots* or a movie like *The Day After* was.

A final factor in evaluating TV movies today is that their success has caused them to proliferate in ways that give us pause. For every serious movie we see, there are five or ten overnight travesties of some sensational headline story. The level of sensationalism is far greater now than it was earlier, and the speed and tastelessness with which movies about disasters, scandals, and tragedies are produced is alarming. This is not to say that even these movies do not often have merit, of the same kind found in such early sensational movies as *Little Ladies of the Night*, about a teenage runaway. But the tasteless and incoherent blockbusters are ever more common.

What does this situation tell us about the role of TV movies in our lives? Have they lost their particular political significance? It is a hard question. What is happening in television is no different from what is happening throughout the media world: a proliferation of cultural products produced for and consumed by people in more and more varied ways. In a postmodern age, this differentiation of audiences and modes of reception is inevitable.

Nonetheless, one might argue that this very situation has worked to increase the networks' concern with creating blockbusters, major media events. Much as the Hollywood studios moved toward major extravaganzas with very high budgets as a way of differentiating themselves from and competing with television, so the networks are doing much the same thing because of cable and video.

The need for centrally mediated "events" through which to enable public discourse on major controversial issues has not changed. The media, as a unified entity, still colludes in an effort to maintain as strong a semblance of national presence as possible. The world of multinational media conglomerates is hardly one of pure competition. It has interests in common with other institutions of power based on the most basic economic partnerships, as well as a common need to maintain a common hegemony based on the common interests of all of its major players.

The intertextual nature of all media works to assure that texts produced in one place will be referred to and hailed by others. The larger world of media thus serves to work in very amiable ways. The network interests are shared by the other media. Television viewing, like all other forms of media consumption, is correlated with other forms of cultural activity. Those who watch the most TV also buy the most books. Tie-ins with products—Smurf toys and books, for example—are now common. And TV movies will certainly develop in ways that increasingly tie them into this intertextual network.

The issue of national politics is another matter. Will we see more and more reactionary telefeatures? Is the age of *The Burning Bed* gone? Clearly, television reflects the conservatizing trends of the nation as a whole. Family sitcoms devoid of political content dominate, along with the revival of such conservative forms as Westerns.

Still, the role of the TV movie has always been to stand out as different and to at least seem to be serious and provocative. This will not change. The very existence of a movie like *Roe v. Wade* indicates as much. It was produced in the most audacious manner possible, against the grain of every dominant political tendency. If there is any place on television where controversy and oppositional voices will continue to be heard, it is TV movies. That is what they were developed for and what they have been increasingly molded to provide.

Moreover, the wave of baby-boom-generation TV workers assures that the voices of middle-class liberalism will not be drowned out. The conservatives have always been right about the left-liberal slant of creative people in television. The arts draw progressives, and television, for better or worse, is where most of the jobs are. If a series like "Twin Peaks" fails to survive, that speaks even more strongly for the strength of the one-shot program as an opportunity to present controversy and non-hegemonic views.

Afterword

It is important to pay attention to this genre, then. In a world in which serious representation and discourse are hard to find, TV movies remain an intriguing communicative arena within which meanings and values that affect us as a nation are struggled over and defined.

Bibliography

Allen, Robert C. *Speaking of Soap Operas*. Chapel Hill and London, 1985.

_____. *Channels of Discourse: Television and Contemporary Criticism*. Chapel Hill, 1987.

Ang, Ien. *Watching Dallas: Soap Opera and the Melodramatic Imagination*. London and New York, 1985.

_____. *Desperately Seeking the Audience*. London and New York, 1991.

Bagdikian, Ben. *The Media Monopoly*. Boston, 1983.

Barnouw, Erik. *Tube of Plenty*. New York, 1975.

_____. *The Sponsor: Notes on a Modern Potentate*. New York, 1978.

Barthes, Roland. *S/Z*. New York, 1974.

_____. *Mythologies*. New York, 1975.

Bennett, Tony, Susan Boyd-Bowman, Colin Mercer, and Janet Wollacott, eds. *Popular Television and Film*. London, 1981.

Bordwell, David, and Kristin Thompson. *Film Art*. Madison, 1986.

Bourdieu, Pierre. *Distinction: A Social Critique of the Judgment of Taste*. Cambridge, 1981.

Brooks, Tim, and Earle Marsh. *The Complete Directory to Prime Time: Network Television Shows, 1946–Present*. New York, 1985.

Browne, Nick. "The Political Economy of the Television (Super)Text." *Quarterly Review of Film Studies* 9, no. 3 (1984) 585–600.

Brunsdon, Charlotte. "Television: Aesthetics and Audiences." In *Logics of Television: Essays in Cultural Criticism*, ed. Patricia Mellencamp, 59–72. Bloomington, 1990.

Cantor, Muriel. *Prime Time Television and Control*. Beverly Hills, 1980.

Carpenter, Teresa. "Crime as Entertainment." *Village Voice*, January 2, 1990: 2–9.

Caughie, John. "Progressive Television and Documentary Drama." In *Popular Television and Film*, ed. Tony Bennett, Susan Boyd-Bowman, Colin Mercer, and Janet Wollacott, 327–53. London, 1981.

_____. "Playing at Being American: Games and Tactics." In *Logics of Television*, ed. Patricia Mellencamp. Bloomington, 1990.

Chodorow, Nancy. *The Reproduction of Mothering: Psychoanalysis and the Sociology of Gender*. Berkeley, 1978.

151

Bibliography

Collins, Jim. *Uncommon Cultures: Popular Culture and Post-Modernism.* New York and London, 1989.

Czitrom, Daniel. *Media and the American Mind: From Morse to McLuhan.* Chapel Hill, 1982.

D'Acci, Julie. "The Case of Cagney and Lacey." In *Boxed In: Women and Television,* ed. Helen Baehr and Gillian Dyer. London, 1987.

de Certeau, Michel. *The Practice of Everyday Life,* trans. Steven Rendall. Berkeley, 1984.

de Lauretis, Teresa. *Alice Doesn't: Feminism, Semiotics, Cinema.* Bloomington, 1984.

———. *Technologies of Gender: Essays on Theory, Film and Fiction.* Bloomington, 1987.

Doane, Mary Ann, Patricia Mellencamp, and Linda Williams, eds. *Re-Vision: Essays in Feminist Film Criticism.* Frederick, Va., 1984.

Earley, Steven. *An Introduction to American Movies.* New York, 1978.

Eley, Geoff. "Nations, Publics, and Political Cultures: Placing Habermas in the Nineteenth Century." In *Habermas and the Public Sphere,* ed. Craig Calhoun. Cambridge, 1991.

Ellis, John. *Visible Fictions.* London, 1982.

Ewen, Elizabeth, and Stuart Ewen. *Channels of Desire.* New York, 1979.

Ewen, Stuart. *Captains of Consciousness.* New York, 1976.

———. *All Consuming Images.* New York, 1989.

Farber, Stephen. "Making Books on Television." *Film Comment,* November 1983: 4–9.

Feuer, Jane. "MTM Enterprises: An Overview." In *MTM "Quality Television,"* ed. Jane Feuer, Paul Kerr, and Tise Vahimagi. London, 1984.

———. "Narrative Form in American Network Television." In *High Theory/Low Culture,* ed. Colin MacCabe, 101–14. New York, 1986.

Fishbein, Leslie. "*Roots*: Docudrama and the Interpretation of History." In *American History/American Television: Interpreting the Video Past,* ed. John E. O'Connor. New York, 1983.

Fiske, John. "Television: Polysemy and Popularity." *Critical Studies in Mass Communication* 3, no. 4 (1986): 391–408.

———. *Television Culture.* London and New York, 1987.

———. "Popular Narrative and Commercial Television." *Camera Obscura,* May 1990: 133–48.

Foner, Eric. "The Inside Story of TV's *Roots.*" *Sevendays,* March 1977: 263–66.

Fraser, Nancy. "Rethinking the Public Sphere." *Social Text* 8, no. 3/9, no. 1 (25/26, 1991): 56–80.

Gamman, Lorraine, and Margaret Marshment. *The Female Gaze: Women As Viewers of Popular Culture.* Seattle, 1989.

Gerber, David A. "Haley's *Roots* and Our Own: An Enquiry into the Nature of a Popular Phenomenon." *Journal of Ethnic Studies,* Fall 1977: 6–9.

Giannetti, Louis. *Understanding Movies.* Englewood Cliffs, N. J., 1987.

Gitlin, Todd. *Inside Prime Time.* New York, 1984.

Gledhill, Christine. "The Melodramatic Field: An Investigation." In *Home Is Where the Heart Is: Studies in Melodrama and the Woman's Film,* ed. Christine Gledhill. London, 1987.

Gomery, Douglas. "*Brian's Song*: Television, Hollywood, and the Evolution of the

Bibliography

Movie Made for Television." In *American History/American Television: Interpreting the Video Past,* ed. John E. O'Connor. New York, 1983.

Gordon, Linda. "On 'Difference.' " *Genders* 10 (Spring 1991): 91–111.

Grant, Barry Keith. "Experience and Meaning in Genre Film." In *Film Genre Reader,* ed. Barry Keith Grant, 114–29. Austin, 1986.

Gray, Ann. "Behind Closed Doors: Video Recorders in the Home." In *Boxed In: Women and Television,* ed. Helen Baehr and Gillian Dyer, 38–55. London, 1989.

Greenwald, Robert. Unpublished interview with the author, 1985.

Grossberg, Lawrence. "I'd Rather Feel Bad Than Not Feel Anything at All." *Enclitic* 8 (Spring/Fall 1984): 95–103.

Hall, Stuart. "Encoding/Decoding." In *Culture, Media, Language,* ed. Stuart Hall, Dorothy Hobson, Andrew Lowe, and Paul Willis, 128–38. London, 1980.

_____. "Cultural Studies: Two Paradigms." In *Culture, Ideology and Social Progress,* ed. Tony Bennett, Graham Martin, Colin Mercer, and Janet Wollacott, 19–28. London, 1981.

_____. "The Rediscovery of Ideology: Return of the Repressed in Media Studies." In *Culture, Society and the Media,* ed. Michael Gurevitch, Tony Bennett, James Curren, and James Wollacott, 59–90. London, 1982.

_____. "The Emergence of Cultural Studies and the Crisis of the Humanities." *October* 8 (Summer 1990): 11–24.

Haraway, Donna. "Overhauling the Media Machines: An Interview with Donna Haraway." Conducted by Marcy Darnovsky. *Socialist Review* 21, no. 2 (April-June 1991): 65–84.

Hobson, Dorothy. "Now That I'm Married." In *Feminism for Girls: An Adventure Story,* ed. Angela McRobbie and Trisha McCabe, 101–12. London, 1981.

_____. *Crossroads: The Drama of a Soap Opera.* London, 1982.

Huyssen, Andreas. *After the Great Divide: Modernism, Mass Culture, Postmodernism.* Bloomington, 1986.

Jameson, Fredric. *Marxism and Form: Twentieth Century Dialectical Theories of Literature.* New York, 1971.

_____. "Reification and Utopia in Mass Culture." *Social Text* 1 (1979): 130–48.

_____. *The Political Unconscious.* Ithaca, N.Y., 1981.

Jarvik, Lawrence, and Nancy Strickland. "TV Movies: Better Than the Real Thing." *American Film,* December 1988: 4–6.

Jenkins, Henry. "If I Could Speak with Your Sound: Fan Music, Textual Proximity, and Liminal Identification." *Camera Obscura* 23 (May 1990): 149–77.

Jones, Kathleen B. "The Trouble with Authority." *differences* 5 (Spring 1991): 104–27.

Jones, Louis V. B. "The Postmodern Moment." *New York Times,* July 16, 1989.

Joyrich, Lynn. "All That Television Allows: TV Melodrama, Postmodernism and Consumer Culture." *Camera Obscura* 16 (May 1987): 12–5.

Kaplan, E. Ann. 1987. "Mothering, Feminism and Representation: The Maternal in Melodrama and the Woman's Film, 1910–40." In *Home Is Where the Heart Is: Studies in Melodrama and the Woman's Film,* ed. Christine Gledhill, 113–38. New York and London, 1987.

Kellner, Douglas. "Network Television and American Capitalism." *Theory and Society,* January 1981, 67–81.

Bibliography

_____. "TV, Ideology, and Emancipatory Popular Culture." In *Television: The Critical View,* ed. Horace Newcomb, 470–503. New York and Oxford, 1978.

_____. *Postmodernism, Jameson, Critique.* Washington, D.C., 1989.

Kluge, Alexander. "The Public Sphere and Experience: Selections." *October* 46 (Fall 1988): 60–83.

Kuhn, Annette. *The Power of the Image: Essays on Representation and Sexuality.* London, 1985.

Lewallen, Avis. "Lace: Pornography for Women?" In *The Female Gaze: Women As Viewers of Popular Culture,* ed. by Lorraine Gamman and Margaret Marshment, 86–102. London, 1989.

Lewis, Lisa A. *Gender Politics and MTV: Voicing the Difference.* Philadelphia, 1990.

Liebes, Tamar, and Elihu Katz. "Patterns of Involvement in Television Fiction." *European Journal of Communication* 1 (1986): 151–71.

McArthur, Colin. "Days of Hope." In *Popular Television and Film,* ed. Tony Bennett, Susan Boyd-Bowman, Colin Mercer, and Janet Wollacott. London, 1981.

MacCabe, Colin. *High Theory/Low Culture.* New York, 1986.

McClary, Susan. "Living To Tell: Madonna's Resurrection of the Fleshly." *Genders* Spring 1990: 1–22.

Mann, Patricia. "Unifying Discourse: City College As Postmodern Public Sphere." *Social Text* 8, no. 3/9, no. 1 (25/26, 1990): 81–102.

Marc, David. *Demographic Vistas: Television in American Culture.* Philadelphia, 1984.

Marill, Alvin. *Movies Made for Television: 1964–1986.* New York, 1987.

Mayne, Judith. "Review Essay: Feminist Film Theory and Criticism." *Signs* 2 (1985): 81–100.

Modleski, Tania. *Loving with a Vengeance: Mass-Produced Fantasies for Women.* New York and London, 1982.

_____. *Studies in Entertainment: Critical Approaches to Mass Culture.* Bloomington, 1986.

Monaco, James. *Media Culture.* New York, 1978.

Morley, David. *Family Television: Cultural Power and Domestic Leisure.* London, 1987.

Morris, Meaghan. "Banality in Cultural Studies." In *Logics of Television,* ed. Patricia Mellencamp, 14–44. Bloomington, 1990.

Mulvey, Laura. "Visual Pleasure and Narrative Cinema." In *Women and the Cinema,* edited by Karyn Kay and Gerald Peary, 409–20. New York, 1977.

_____. "Notes on Sirk and Melodrama." In *Home Is Where the Heart Is: Studies in Melodrama and the Woman's Film,* ed. Christine Gledhill, 75–83. London, 1987.

Nielsen Media Research. *1988 Report on Television.* New York.

_____. *Perspective on Working Women.* New York, 1988.

_____. *Total Women/Working Women Viewing Study.* New York, 1988.

O'Connor, John E. *American History/American Television: Interpreting the Video Past.* New York, 1983.

Powers, Ron. *The Newscasters.* New York, 1977.

Preiss, Andrea. *Women Watching Television: Gender, Class and Generation in the American Television Experience.* Philadelphia, 1991.

Radway, Janice. *Reading the Romance: Women, Patriarchy and Popular Literature.* Chapel Hill, N. C., 1984.

Bibliography

Rapping, Elayne. "The View from Hollywood: The American Family and the American Dream." *Socialist Review*, January-February 1983: 71–93.

———. "TV Movies: The Domestication of Social Issues." *Cineaste*, Fall 1985: 10–17.

———. *The Looking Glass World of Nonfiction Television*. Boston, 1987.

———. "Teen Cult Films." *Cineaste* 19, no. 3 (1988): 14–21.

———. "TV Guides." *Voice Literary Supplement*, December 1990: 5.

Russ, Joanna. "Somebody's Trying to Kill Me and I Think It's My Husband: The Modern Gothic." *Journal of Popular Culture* 6 (1973): 666–91.

Schatz, Thomas. *Hollywood Genres: Formulas, Filmmaking and the Studio System*. Philadelphia, 1981.

Sholle, David. "Resistance: Pinning Down a Wandering Concept in Cultural Studies Discourse." *Journal of Urban and Cultural Studies* 1, no. 1 (1990): 87–107.

Siegenthaler, John. "Remembering the Kennedys." *USA Today*, January 23, 1985.

Sklar, Robert. *Movie-Made America: A Cultural History of American Movies*. New York, 1975.

Spivak, Gayatri. "Criticism, Feminism and the Institution." In *Intellectuals: Aesthetics, Politics, Academics,* ed. Bruce Robbins, 153–72. Minneapolis, 1990.

Steinberg, Cobbett. *TV Facts*. New York, 1980.

Streeter, Thomas. "Polysemy, Plurality and Media Studies." *Critical Studies in Mass Communication Inquiry* 13, no. 11 (1989): 1–33.

Taylor, Ella. *Primetime Families*. Berkeley, Calif., 1989.

Todorov, Tzvetan. *Mikhail Bakhtin: The Dialogical Principle*. Minneapolis, 1984.

Tuchman, Gaye. *Making News: A Study in the Construction of Reality*. New York, 1978.

TV Guide. "Top Rated Shows of the Season." July 8, 1989: 9–15.

Variety. "Hit Movies on U.S. Television Since 1961." January –0, 1989: 40–49.

Wasko, Janet. *Movies and Money: Financing the American Film Industry*. Philadelphia, 1982.

Williams, Linda. " 'Something Else besides a Mother': Stella Dallas and the Maternal Melodrama." *Cinema Journal* 24, no. 1 (Fall 1984): 2–27.

Williams, Raymond. *Television: Technology and Cultural Form*. New York, 1975.

———. *Problems in Materialism and Culture*. London, 1980.

Williamson, Judith. *Consuming Passions: The Dynamics of Popular Culture*. New York, 1985.

Wood, Robin. "Ideology, Genre, Auteur." *Film Comment*, January-February 1977: 274–89.

Index

Compiled by Robin Jackson

Index

Index

Index

Index

Elayne Rapping is a professor of communications at Adelphi University and the author of *The Looking Glass World of Nonfiction Television* and the forthcoming *In These Rooms: Women, Addiction, and the Recovery Movement.* She writes regularly on media and feminism for a variety of publications.